D0196482

PLANTWORKS

PLANTWORKS

A Wild Plant Cookbook, Field Guide and Activity Book

For the Novice & Naturalist

Karen Shanberg and Stan Tekiela

Botanical drawings by Laverne Dunsmore

Other drawings by Tracy L. Gerdin

Photographs by Stan Tekiela

Adventure Publications

Cambridge, Minnesota

1991

Many special thanks to our spouses, Neil and Kathy for their loving support and to Louise Olsen and Jim David for their encouragement and advice.

This book is dedicated to the next generation, our nieces and nephews:

Becca, Meredith, David Arnold, Marissa, Rachel, Brian, Emily, Jessica, Britt, Kimberly, Eric, James, Anna, Samantha, Danny, David, Kyle and Kory.

May they be the inspiration to us all to leave a planet worth inheriting.

© 1991 Adventure Publications, Box 269, Cambridge, MN 55008. All rights reserved. Pages 105-146 may be reproduced for family and nature group use without permission.

Botanical illustrations © 1991 Laverne Dunsmore.
Book and icon design by Nathaniel Case.
Cover design by Paula Roth.

ISBN: 0-934860-70-X

1st Edition, May 1991
10 9 8 7 6 5 4 3 2 1

Printed on Recycled Paper

TABLE OF CONTENTS

Range Map

11 of the 15 Plantworks plants are widespread in one or more
varieties in all 48 contiguous states, except the deep South and
extreme Northeast. Three plants — basswood, stinging nettle and
sumac — are generally not found in the West. Winter Cress is
found in the East and along the West coast.

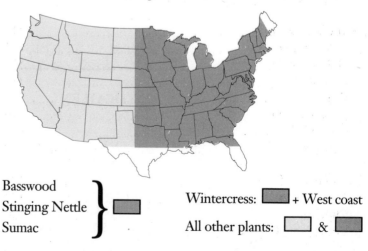

Basswood
Stinging Nettle }
Sumac

Wintercress: [■] + West coast

All other plants: [ ] & [■]

GUIDE TO PLANTWORKS

HABITATS

 OPENLANDS. Dry grassy areas including lawn, disturbed soils, vacant lots and gardens.

 TRANSITION. Shrubby growth areas at the edge or border of lake, forest, stream or prairie habitats, which exhibit characteristics of two different areas.

 WETLAND. Low lying wet areas, sparsely populated with tall reed-like plants often bordering lakes and streams.

 WOODLAND. Areas where the dominant plants are hardwood, deciduous trees as in oak and maple-basswood forests.

 SPRING

 SUMMER

 FALL

 WINTER

 IN THE SKILLET
Stir-fry & Batter Recipes

 IN THE OVEN
Breads, Quiches, etc.

 ON THE STOVE
Teas, Jellies, Soups, etc.

 NO COOKING REQUIRED Salads, Trail Nibbles, Pickles & more

EASY ACCESS GUIDE

	RECIPES	SEASONS	HABITATS
Basswood	p. 74		
Cattail	p. 76		
Curled Dock	p. 78		
Dandelion	p. 80		
Lamb's Quarters	p. 82		
Oak	p. 84		
Plantain	p. 86		
Purslane	p. 88		
Red Clover	p. 90		
Stinging Nettle	p. 92		
Sumac	p. 94		
Wild Grape	p. 96		
Wild Rose	p. 98		
Winter Cress	p. 100		
Yellow Wood Sorrel	p. 102		

FOREWORD

Whether you are a weekend hiker, scout leader, teacher, naturalist, day care provider, parent, or a combination thereof, this book is designed to introduce you and your group to the outdoors by way of your stomach! Our unique recipes are wonderfully tasty compared with any food, not just wild food. Just follow the steps in this book and with ordinary ingredients, a few carefully harvested plants, some basic cooking skills and an open mind you can be a successful wild foods cook.

As a wild foods cook you can impart to those around you sensitivity and respect for *all* that nature has to offer. *Plantworks* will help to fine tune your observation skills as you learn about habitats (where plants live), plant anatomy (the structures of the plants), phenology (when they are in season), and some ecology (how they fit into the scheme of things). All this you can share with the children or other adults in your life.

We encourage cooks and non-cooks, naturalists and novices to use this book as a guide for safely harvesting and preparing plants commonly thought of as weeds. Remember that a weed is just a plant for which we haven't found a use.

Plantworks is more than a wild foods cookbook, it is a way to get people of all ages excited about the world of wild plants. It is critical that we begin to value plants and their life-sustaining elements at an early age. Taking them for granted has led to the destruction of forests and the spreading of deserts at home and around the world.

Earth Day 1990 awakened many of us to the need to eat lower on the food chain. As our world becomes more crowded it is more and more important to use our food resources efficiently by eating more plants and fewer animals raised on plants. *Plantworks* was written to reflect this spirit.

We hope that the ideas of making delicious food from "weeds" will catch on and people will leave more wild areas near their homes in order to keep a ready supply of these plants as a source of food. It is becoming more and more difficult to find areas where wild plants thrive and where picking is allowed. Nature has been relegated to an existence within park boundaries. Roadsides are mowed and lawns are planted where much wildlife once flourished. We would like to see these wild plants viewed in a new way so that their growth would increase habitat for wildlife. In this light, we urge conservative, responsible harvesting. Using some of what nature has to offer implies we are a part of nature too.

We would like to extend our sincere gratitude for their diligent review of this book to: John D. Jackson, Ph. D. Botanical Sciences, of the Biology Department at North Hennepin Community College in Brooklyn Park, MN; Joseph McCulloch, Ph. D. Botanical Sciences, of the Biology Department at Normandale Community College in Bloomington, MN; and Chef Jeff Frederick of Minnetrista, MN.

PREFACE

Here it is, a guide book, cookbook and activity book all rolled into one! *Plantworks* welcomes the novice as well as the seasoned naturalist to sample its recipes and activities.

We have taught many classes on gathering and cooking wild edible plants. Participants in our classes often want to know how they could learn to do the whole process on their own, from gathering to cooking. We have never been able to recommend just one source, so we decided to write a book to include all of the steps in wild food cooking.

To invite all potential wild foods cooks to experience this art, we organized this guide book like a regular cookbook. Do you want to bake, fry, or just eat along the trail with your students? Would you like to make soups, muffins, teas, salads or sweetbreads? Once you have selected a cooking process, find a recipe which strikes your group's fancy. A quick check in the margin of the recipe will tell you if the plant is in season, where it can be located, about how much the recipe will cost and how long it will take. Then read about the plant in the natural history section, hike to the plant, gather just enough for the recipe and cook it.

We have written this book as a guide to help you experience the thrill of harvesting and cooking wild edible plants. The plants we have selected are easy to locate and our creative recipes are easy to use with a group. The suggested activities extend your group's involvement with wild plants and may help to make identifications without mistakes, the first step in any wild edible excursion. *Plantworks* is also for adults without groups, who would like to master another outdoor skill or try some non-traditional recipes. You might think that you have to be planning a trip to the woods in order to collect wild edible plants, but all of the plants in our recipes are common on roadsides, backyards and pond edges. You do not have to be a camper to enjoy the recipes in *Plantworks*, but if you already camp, then learning how to enhance your camping cuisine with the addition of some wild edible plants will make your experience more exciting. *Plantworks* is intended to provide a fun way to get closer to nature through your tastebuds.

Enjoy the wild,

Karen and Stan

PLANTWORKS

To those of you who are teachers, we offer this:

"Do not try to satisfy your vanity by teaching a great many things. Awaken people's curiosity. It is enough to open minds—do not overload them. Put there just a spark. If there is some good inflammable stuff, it will catch fire."

Anatole France

INTRODUCTION

Organizing a Group Outing

This section is devoted to those parents, teachers, naturalists, scout leaders and day care providers who would like a blueprint for leading a wild foods activity with a group of kids. The following activities are written for kids aged 6-16.

GETTING READY: BEFORE THE HIKE

Cooking wild foods helps people become more aware of their natural environment. But to excite kids about "weeds" it's a good idea to promote the eating aspect first. If kitchen facilities are available, ask your group to choose something to cook and then tell them that they have the opportunity to collect some of the ingredients themselves. It is very satisfying to go through the whole process of collecting, cooking and eating a wild plant. The variety of our recipes is intended to have a wide appeal. Don't avoid the cooked greens if you are working with kids. Parents and scout leaders are routinely surprised that their children are eating and enjoying cooked vegetables. Because they are eating something they picked and cooked themselves, their curiosity usually overrides the common juvenile urge to avoid most leafy green things.

After choosing your process (i.e. baking, frying etc.) select a plant readily available in your area whose leaves, fruits or seeds are in season. The natural history section gives you interesting details about the plant you are seeking. Present a slide, print or a recently picked specimen of the chosen plant to your group and ask them to guess which parts of it are edible. As a group, have them generate some rules about harvesting wild plants and see if they come close to the list that follows. Go over these rules several times before the hike.

THE GOLDEN RULES OF HARVESTING WILD PLANTS

First we need to define just what we mean by the term "wild edibles." For the purposes of this book, we will define edible as something which is not harmful to the average healthy person when eaten in reasonable amounts and which is fairly tasty to most people.

We have chosen plants which are commonly found and are so explicitly illustrated that they can be safely chosen by the beginner. The 15 wild edible plants in this book do not have any poisonous parts. Many common garden crops cannot make this claim. For example, both tomato leaves and rhubarb leaves are toxic.

You will need to follow and teach those in your charge the following rules:

1) Always be 110% sure of the identification of the plant you are picking. Leave careless experimentation to the foolhardy.

2) Select only healthy plants. Look for insects and other small herbivores before selecting your leaves.

3) Choose the young green leaves of the edible plants. Many leaves develop a chemical called "tannin" and become bitter with age.

4) Apply the rule of 10: harvest only one plant to every 10 that you leave behind. Usually it is not necessary to take the whole plant, root and all. Removing a few leaves, petals, fruits or seeds from several plants is better than taking all you need from one plant.

5) Harvest only what you will need for your recipe. Too much of even a healthy plant may make you sick because it is new to your system.

6) Harvest only the edible parts of a plant that are ripe. Out of season edibles can be very bitter.

7) Dismiss all rules of harvesting which begin with a sentence like "All blue berries are edible...." There are no across-the-board rules for distinguishing edible from poisonous plants.

8) If one plant in a botanical family is edible, it does not mean that all plants in the family are edible. Conversely, if a plant is poisonous it does not mean that all related plants are poisonous.

9) Sometimes, only a special part of a plant is edible. The rest may be indigestible or even poisonous (none of the Plantworks plants have poisonous parts).

10) Be knowledgeable about the area you've selected for harvesting. Is it part of a park? Is it owned by the county? You'll want to know if herbicides or pesticides have been used there. If you aren't sure, call a local county or state official and ask. Besides finding the information you need, you will let government officials know you are concerned about chemical sprays.

THE HARVEST

First, select a recipe which uses a plant currently in season. Locate the plant in the natural history section, study the illustration and read the information to be sure of your identification.

Bring *Plantworks* with you outdoors to use as a field guide. Select a secluded area where you can sit down and read about the plant once again before you continue your hike. The harvest is most fun when your group is excited about locating a potential delectable. The only equipment that you'll need includes proper foot gear, a bucket, a pocketknife and a pair of garden gloves (essential for stinging nettles). Use the illustrations and photos to help you confirm your identification.

Insist on proper clothing to make sure that your group doesn't lose enthusiasm for hiking. Hats are always an asset in keeping away bugs and sunshine and drizzle. We recommend long pants, socks and sturdy shoes for all temperatures. Avoiding abrasions, ticks and mosquitoes is well worth the extra warmth long pants may bring.

The phrase, "step lightly on the Earth," teaches us to respect the systems of our planet and to use its resources with thoughts of the future. The hike to pick plants is a great opportunity to teach this concept. Wild edible hikes can teach people to value plants and the areas in which they grow. The most important aspect of the hike is to create a mood for listening and looking rather than a playground attitude of running and yelling.

Don't be intimidated by all of the questions you get for which you don't immediately know the answers. Make notes and later use this as an opportunity to teach children how to use books or a local nature center as a resource.

Children benefit from learning to notice the patterns, sights and smells of the natural world. As their world gets more and more urbanized, there is little opportunity for them to naturally develop these skills. Point out an insect along the way. It doesn't matter if you know its name, but observe its behavior and notice its shape. Is it eating the leaf it's on? Is it camouflaged to match the leaf or brightly colored to warn of its poisonous nature? Which way is the wind blowing? Do the clouds forecast rain? Observations like these are very significant for the children. Technical names of insects, plants and clouds can be acquired later. First arouse their curiosity through their senses. Refer to the activity pages for more specific ideas of what to do on your hike.

SOMEONE'S IN THE KITCHEN

Let everyone have a chance to help in the cooking by taking turns to mix batter, fry fritters or spoon muffins, etc. When working in a group, it is most convenient to set up cooking stations. For younger children, have each ingredient and correct measuring cup or spoon laid out on the table at a workable height. It is easiest to divide up the baking recipes into "wet" and "dry" ingredients. Put all of those in charge of a dry ingredient (flour, baking powder etc.) on one side of the working area and those responsible for wet ingredients (milk, egg etc.) on the other, each side with its own large mixing bowl. Explain all directions before letting anyone begin. Measuring accurately is a good skill to pick up at an early age. You also have an opportunity to teach about fractions, especially if you are going to double a recipe or cut one in half.

Those who finish early can clean up and set the table. Use washable plates, cups and forks when you serve food to your group. Though

.lean-up may not be as convenient, disposable plates and plastic-ware waste resources and use limited landfill space. Children will accept washing the dishes rather than throwing them away when they see how this choice is so much more respectful of the Earth and her limited resources. It will be that much more respectful if the water doesn't run constantly during the process. Take a minute to show those with K.P. duty how to save water by using a soapy sponge to clean the dishes and then rinse them. The process of cleaning up the kitchen after cooking is another opportunity to be more environmentally aware. Choose biodegradable soaps in re-cycled or recyclable containers.

WHILE YOU WAIT

You may want to copy and hand out pencil and paper activities from the activity section while you wait for your food to cook or bake. Or you might choose to begin one of these activities and finish it after you eat. Watch the food carefully so it isn't under- or over-cooked as many children (and adults) object to both.

Tasting the food is the highlight for the group, and they should begin eating together. Children are very influenced by their peers, and an unfavorable response by one may discourage others from even trying your recipe. If you have the time, prepare other tradi-tional foods to eat along with the wild food choice to give the students the impression that this plant recipe can be a part of any meal. Have them evaluate the meal and impress upon them the importance of picking and eating wild plants only when a knowl-edgeable adult is present. To reinforce their memory of the plants they ate, do one or some of the follow-up Extended Activities.

EXTENDED ACTIVITIES

After the hiking, harvesting, cooking and eating, you can begin the process all over again with another plant or you can extend the activity even longer by planning a wild edible plant-related craft from the Extended Activities section. The crafts will make your group's wild edible experience more memorable as they will have something to show their family and friends. Try these additional ideas to extend the entire wild edible cooking experience:

- After trying several recipes you can construct a graph or chart indicating the group's favorite recipes.

- Decorate a recipe box and include your favorite wild food recipes to give as a gift.

- Design a poster promoting wild plant habitats.

- Learn about several endangered wild plants in your area.

- Invite a speaker from the local Nature Conservancy or native plant society to come and talk to your group.

- Make a video-tape of a well-rehearsed cooking session and show it to others.

- Have a wild foods tasting party for your friends and relatives.

- Press an example of each plant in Plantworks so that you may safely harvest it at any time. (See p. 144 on how to make a pocket plant press).

- Make a poster of a simplified version of the rule of harvesting wild plants.

- Get involved in supporting the conservation efforts in your local community. If someone is trying to preserve a wetland, prairie or forest in your area, perhaps your group can help.

HOW TO DRY PLANTS

for long term storage

The drying process is simple yet essential for storing plants for later use. Several different processes can be used to achieve dryness in plant material for long-term storage:

The paper bag method: This is by far the easiest method. No special equipment is needed; in fact, all you need is a paper bag and a refrigerator. Collect the plant part that is to be dried. Fill the paper bag only half full and roll the top closed. Place the bag in the refrigerator and check on it every couple of days until dry. This process should take no longer than five days.

The food dehydrator method: A food dehydrator (p. 142) will dry large amounts of plant material faster, but will obviously take some time to build. Dehydrators can also be purchased at over twice the cost of building one. Once the dryer has been built you can dry just about any plant in 6 to 12 hours. It is well worth the time and effort to build this dehydrator.

The oven-drying method: Oven-drying is fast, but great care must be taken to avoid burning. The oven door should be left open and the oven set at the lowest possible setting. Spread out the material on a cookie sheet and place on the middle oven rack. This is not a process that can be left unattended. Watch closely and stir the material frequently to allow even drying. If any part of the material burns, remove it and throw it away.

Air-drying method: All plant material in small amounts can be dried on ordinary window screens laid out flat and kept in a cool dry place out of the sun. Spread out the material to be dried and check for dryness every day or so.

Hanging method: A whole plant can be dried by cutting it at its base and hanging it upside-down in a cool, dry place. This process will take several weeks. Once dried, the plants can be left hanging or can be stored in glass jars.

Storage: Storing is as easy as pouring the dried plant materials into a glass jar and sealing. The key here is the dryness of the material; *any* moisture will cause mold and fungal growth. If signs of these growths appear, throw the material away; it is useless. Thoroughly dried material will last years in sealed glass jars, extending the fun of wild edibles all year long!

RECIPES

 In the Skillet *(pages 13-21)*
Stir-fry and batter-fry recipes

 In the Oven *(pages 22-32)*
Muffins, breads, quiche and more

 On the Stove *(pages 33-56)*
Teas, jellies, soups and vegetables

 No Cooking Required *(pages 57-70)*
Salads, pickles and trail nibbles

Cooking foods from scratch eliminates the need to buy prepared foods in wasteful packaging. About half of the paper in the United States—and 11% of the aluminum—goes into packaging. Whenever possible, buy ingredients in bulk and store them in reusable containers.

When buying groceries (especially in small amounts), use reusable cloth or mesh bags to carry them home, or at least find uses for the paper bags before throwing them away.

Cook on a gas stove if possible. Gas energy is more efficient and cleaner for the environment than electricity, which is usually generated by oil- or coal-burning or nuclear power plants, or by hydroelectric dams. A stove with an electronic starter will save 40% of the gas used by a pilot-light range. Keeping your burners and pilot light clean will save energy because they will burn more efficiently.

PLANTWORKS RECIPE KEY

Each Plantworks recipe comes with a key which will tell you at a glance the following information:

COOKING METHOD- See guide on p. 11

WHEN- When the part of the plant featured in the recipe can be found in season.

WHERE- Location/habitat of the plant. This will be a choice of woodland, openland, transition or wetland. The definitions of these areas are listed on p. ix.

COST- Approximate cost for making one recipe. Ingredient costs will be under $2.00, $5.00, $10.00, or $15.00 to make.

TIME- The approximate time it takes to prepare one recipe. This does not include the time needed to harvest ingredients or to wait for baking or chilling.

PLANT- The name of the plant used in the recipe and the Natural History page where its illustration and information about locating it can be found.

ACTIVITIES- The page number of the Extended Activities which particularly pertain to the plant featured in the recipe.

Use this easy reference information to select a recipe suitable to your situation.

IN THE SKILLET

Recipes that you stir fry and batter fry

Frying pans and hot oil can be dangerous and every precaution should be taken to keep children from accidentally touching or tipping hot pans. Be sure cords are inaccessible to prevent tripping over them.

Here are some additional tips to help you have problem-free experiences when you fry with your kids:

- Use a non-stick skillet (frying pan) or wok.

- When you fry using a batter, fry in 1/4-1/2 inch of oil.

- When you fry without a batter, use 2 tbsps of oil per 2 cups of food.

- Use a lid when frying with a batter. Leave the lid off when frying only in oil.

- For added safety when frying with kids, use a low flame or select low temperatures (250° is about right). The frying will take longer, but it will spatter less.

- Electric fry pans are portable and make a wild edible cooking experience easy to do in non-kitchen areas like classrooms.

ACORN PANCAKES

When

Where

Cost

UNDER
$5

Time

30
MINS

Ingredients

1 cup	acorn flour (see p. 23)
1 cup	white flour
2 tbsps	sugar
3 tsps	double action baking powder
1/2 tsp	salt
2	eggs
2 tbsps	vegetable oil
1 1/2 cups	milk
	maple syrup

Directions

Sift together the flour, sugar, salt and baking powder. Whisk the eggs, milk and oil together. Add the dry ingredients while mixing into a medium thick batter. Fry in a greased fry pan as you would for regular pancakes. Serve hot with maple syrup.

Notes

Serves 2-4.

Plant:
Oak tree
pp. 84-85

Activities:
*pp. 122, 124,
134, 140*

ACORN FRY BREAD

Ingredients

1 cup	acorn flour (see p. 23)
1 cup	white flour
1 1/2 tsps	baking powder
1 tsp	salt
1 tsp	vegetable oil
	water
	white flour for kneading
	vegetable oil for frying
	brown sugar

When

Where

Cost
UNDER
$5

Time
30
MINS.

Directions

Sift together the flour, baking powder and salt. Add oil and while mixing together add enough water to make a soft dough. Pull off a ball about the size of a golf ball and knead on a floured counter top. Roll the dough about 1/4" thick. In a large frying pan, heat 1/4 to 1/2" oil. Lay the flat bread in this hot oil and fry once on each side until puffy and brown. Remove. While still hot, sprinkle with brown sugar and allow the sugar to melt. Serve warm.

Notes

It is very important to be careful with the hot oil. If you use a lower heat the bread will not become puffy but rather become oil-soaked and unpleasant.

Plant:
Oak tree
pp. 84-85

Activities:
pp. 122, 124,
134, 140

CATTAIL-VEGETABLE STIR-FRY

Cost
UNDER
$10

Time
30
MINS.

Ingredients

12	cattail stalks (peeled sliced white centers)
1 cup	carrots sliced
2 cups	mushrooms, chopped
2 cups	broccoli, chopped
1	whole green pepper
2 tbsps	soy sauce
1 cup	cold water
3 tbsps	corn starch
	instant brown or white rice
	salt and pepper to taste

Directions

Cook the instant rice according to package instructions. In a wok or a large fry pan heat 3-4 tbsps oil until hot. Stir-fry the carrot and broccoli for 2-3 minutes. The green pepper can be added now or later depending on how crunchy you want the pepper to be. Next add the mushrooms and cattail pieces. Stir constantly for 4-5 minutes. Have the corn starch, soy sauce and water mixed together. Add the liquid to the wok or pan and stir the vegetables until coated with the sauce. Continue cooking for 4-5 minutes, longer for less crunchy vegetables. Serve mixture over a bed of rice.

Plant:
Cattail
pp. 76-77

Activities:
pp. 129, 136, 146

Notes

You can use any combination of your favorite vegetables in this recipe. It's important to use cold water when mixing the corn starch. Whisk it well to avoid lumps. Serves 3-4.

FRESH FRITTERED FLOWERS

Ingredients

2 cups	fresh dandelion flowers
1	egg
1 cup	milk
1 cup	flour
1 tbsp	baking powder
1 tsp	nutmeg
1 tbsp	sugar
	vegetable oil

Directions

Wash flower tops and shake off excess water. Mix together the egg, milk, nutmeg and sugar. Mix flour and baking powder and stir in the liquid mixture until a medium thick batter is made. Dip the flowers into the batter. In a large frying pan add oil to a depth of 1/4". Use medium heat to avoid excess splashing. Cook the flowers until brown, turning them often to cook evenly. Remove and sprinkle with sugar while still hot.

Notes

Kids love to dip the flowers in the batter but need to be supervised when working around the hot oil. It's best to use a medium heat: it takes a little longer to cook, but is much safer.

Serves 4.

Plant:
Dandelion
pp. 80-81

Activities:
pp. 129, 138

SAUTÉED PURSLANE

When

Where

Cost
UNDER
$5

Time
30
MINS

Ingredients

3-5 cups	purslane stems and leaves, washed well
1	large onion, chopped
2 tbsps	oil (peanut oil is preferable)
1 cup	sharp cheddar cheese, grated

Directions

In a skillet, sauté the onions and purslane until tender. Remove from heat and sprinkle on the cheese and allow to melt. If you have any trouble melting the cheese, transfer to a microwave-safe dish and microwave until melted. A broiler can also be used. Serve hot.

Notes

Serves 2-3.

*Plant:
Purslane
pp. 88-89*

*Activity:
p. 131*

LUCKY RED CLOVER FRITTERS

Ingredients

2 cups	red clover flowers
1	egg
1 cup	flour
1 cup	milk
1 tbsp.	baking powder
3/4 tsp.	nutmeg
1 tbsp	sugar
	vegetable oil
optional	*brown or powdered sugar*

Directions

Wash flower tops and shake off the extra water. Mix together the egg, milk, nutmeg and sugar. Mix flour and baking powder and stir in the liquid mixture until a medium batter is made. Heat 1/4" oil in a large frying pan over medium heat. Dip flowers into batter and cook in hot oil until brown. Sprinkle with sugar and serve hot.

Notes

Serves 4.

When

Where

Cost

UNDER
$5

Time

30
MINS

Plant:
Red Clover
pp. 90-91

Activities:
pp. 132, 138

KATHY'S SWEET SUMAC CHICKEN

Ingredients

1/2 cup	sumac syrup (Made the same way as sumac jelly [p. 51] without the pectin added)
2	boneless skinless chicken breasts
3 tbsps	butter
1	large pear cubed
	salt and pepper
	cottage cheese

Directions

Melt the butter in a skillet. Salt and pepper the thawed chicken and cook on both sides over a medium high heat until the chicken starts to brown. Add the cubed pears and cover with the sumac syrup. Stir constantly and lower the heat to avoid burning. Be sure to coat the chicken with the syrup while you are stirring. It's ready when the syrup starts to crystallize. Serve with a side dish of cottage cheese or add champagne for a fancy brunch.

Notes

The trick to this recipe is the sumac syrup. All that is needed is to follow the jelly recipe (p. 51) and omit the pectin, which makes it jell. Be sure not to overcook once the syrup has been added.

Serves 2.

Plant:
Sumac
pp. 94-95

Activities:
pp. 127, 138

SHRIMP AND SORREL STIR-FRY

Ingredients

2 cups	wood sorrel, leaves and stems
1/4 lb	medium shrimp, peeled and deveined
1 small	onion, sliced
1 cup	mushrooms
1/2 cup	pineapple chunks
1	green pepper, chopped
4 tbsps	sesame oil
2 tsps	soy sauce
2 tsps	water
2 tsps	cornstarch
	dash of Tabasco (optional)
	white or brown rice

When

Where

Directions

Stir fry sauce: In a small bowl, mix the corn starch and cold water until the corn starch is dissolved. Add in the soy sauce and a dash of tabasco. Mix well.

Prepare rice as directed. Heat oil to a medium high heat. Toss in shrimp and onions. Stir for 2-4 minutes. Add green pepper, pineapple, mushrooms and stir fry for another 4 minutes. Add the stir fry sauce and wood sorrel (as the last vegetable). Stir just long enough to coat all the ingredients with the sauce. Don't overcook the wood sorrel. Serve on a bed of rice.

Time

1
HOUR

Cost

UNDER
$15

Plant:
Yellow Wood
Sorrel
pp. 102-103

Notes

Serves 2-4. Recipe can be doubled.

Activity:
p. 129

IN THE OVEN

Muffins, breads, quiches and more

Here are some suggestions for a trouble-free excursion into the world of baking:

- Make sure to pre-heat the oven.

- Invest in an oven thermometer which you can put directly into your oven. This is much more accurate than your built-in oven thermometer.

- Use insulated hot pads; burns may occur if you rely on the thinner ones.

- No paper inserts are necessary when baking muffins. They stick often and create waste.

- Consider using a toaster oven, especially for smaller groups. They are portable, convenient and use less energy than conventional ovens.

- Grease pans with margarine or vegetable shortening rather than aerosol sprays. Even though ozone-depleting CFC's (chlorofluorocarbons) will soon no longer be used as propellants, most use air-polluting hydrocarbons. The empty aerosol cans are also a solid waste problem, being non-recyclable.

- Avoid using aerosol sprays when cleaning the oven. In addition to the problems mentioned above, these often contain toxic lye. Instead, moisten the surface with water, sprinkle with baking soda, and scrub the tough spots with fine steel wool.

HOW TO MAKE ACORN FLOUR

Making acorn flour isn't difficult. Gather the acorns beginning in late summer. If you can't process the acorns right away, you should store them in your freezer. Shelling or husking is the most difficult and time-consuming of the steps involved. The task can be made more enjoyable by sitting down with a large bucket, nut cracker and some good friends and talking the night away while you shell the nuts.

Once the acorns have been shelled you need to boil them to remove tannins. Bring a large kettle of water to a boil and pour in the shelled nuts. Boil for 10-15 minutes. While doing this, start a second kettle of water boiling. Once the acorns have boiled in the first pot the water needs to be drained and the acorns put into the second pot of fresh boiling water. This process is repeated over again for 4 changes of water, each lasting 10-15 minutes. Fill the pitcher of a blender half full with acorns and barely cover with fresh warm water. Grind until a thick brown mud is formed. If you don't use enough water the blender will slow and not grind well. Pour this acorn paste into a colander lined with cheesecloth to drain the water. Squeeze the cheesecloth to remove any excess water.

Dry the resulting paste in a food dehydrator you made from the activity section (see p. 142). Alternatively, dry the flour in a oven; spread out the paste on a cookie sheet, set your oven on the lowest possible setting and prop open the door. Depending on the method and equipment used, drying can take from three hours to three days. The outcome will be dry brown chips of acorn flour. Grind up the chips in a blender and store the flour in glass jars. It is very important to have very dry flour or it will mold during storage. Dried flour will store up to a year.

JELLY-FILLED ACORN MUFFINS

When

Where

Cost

UNDER
$10

Time

45
MINS.

Ingredients

1 cup	acorn flour (see p. 23)
1 cup	white flour
1/2 tsp	salt
2 tbsps	sugar
1 cup	milk
1	egg, lightly beaten
3 tbsps	vegetable oil
	your favorite jam or fruit spread

Directions

Combine dry ingredients. Mix together the milk, egg, and oil. In a large bowl mix the dry and wet ingredients together. Grease a muffin tin. Pre-heat oven to 400°. Pour in enough batter to fill the bottom 1/3 of each tin. Spoon in a tbsp of your favorite flavor of jam. Pour in additional batter to fill each tin up to 3/4 full. Bake for 20-25 minutes. Sprinkle some sugar on top when hot out of the oven.

Notes

Makes 8-12 muffins depending on the size of the muffin tin. We don't recommend paper muffin liners as they are a poor use of natural resources and the muffins tend to stick to the paper.

Plant:
Oak tree
pp. 84-85

Activities:
*pp. 122, 127,
134, 140*

ACORN SWEET BREAD

Ingredients

1 cup	acorn flour (see p. 23)
1 cup	wheat flour
2 tsps	baking powder
1/2 tsp	baking soda
1 cup	milk
2 tbsps	oil
1 tsp	vanilla extract
3/4 cup	honey
1	egg, lightly beaten
	butter or shortening to grease bread tin

When

Where

Cost
UNDER $10

Time
1 HOUR

Directions

Combine dry ingredients. Combine wet ingredients. Mix wet and dry ingredients together until a smooth batter is formed. Grease bread tin and pour in the batter. Bake at 375° in a pre-heated oven for 35-40 minutes. Be careful to bake completely. Using honey requires a little more baking time than similar recipes without honey.

Notes

Makes 1 loaf. Serves up to 6.

Plant:
Oak tree
pp. 84-85

Activities:
pp. 122, 127,
134, 140

CURLED DOCK SWEET BREAD

When

Where

Cost
UNDER
$10

Time
1
HOUR

Ingredients

1 cup	curled dock flour*
1 cup	white flour
2 tsps	baking powder
1/2 tsp	baking soda
1 cup	milk
2 tbsps	oil
1 tsp	vanilla extract
1	egg, lightly beaten
3/4 cup	honey
	butter or shortening to grease bread tin

Directions

 Combine dry ingredients in a large bowl. Combine wet ingredients in large bowl. Mix the wet and dry ingredients together until a smooth batter forms. Grease a bread tin and pour in the batter. Bake at 375° in a pre-heated oven for 35 to 40 minutes. Be sure to bake completely as honey requires a little additional time over similar recipes using sugar.

Notes

* See Natural History section (p. 79) for instructions to make curled dock flour.

Makes 1 loaf. Serves up to 6.

Plant:
Curled Dock
pp. 78-79

Activity:
p. 129

CURLED DOCK
RAISIN MUFFINS

Ingredients

1 cup	curled dock flour*
1 cup	wheat flour
1/2 tsp	salt
2 tbsps	sugar
1 cup	milk
1	egg, lightly beaten
3 tbsps	vegetable oil
1 cup	raisins
	sugar to sprinkle on-top

When

Directions

Combine the dry ingredients. Mix milk, egg and oil together and add the dry ingredients. Stir to a stiff batter. Add raisins. Preheat oven to 400°. Grease muffin tins, fill about 2/3 full and bake for 25 to 30 minutes. Test with a toothpick. Sprinkle with sugar while still hot.

Where

Cost

Notes

* See Natural History section (p. 79) for instructions to make curled dock flour.

Makes approximately 1 dozen muffins.

Time

Plant:
Curled Dock
pp. 78-79

Activity:
p. 129

DANDELION CHOCOLATE COFFEE

When

Where

Cost

UNDER $5

Time

1 HOUR

Ingredients

6-10	dandelion roots
	kettle of water
	tea ball
1/2 packet	instant hot chocolate mix (8 oz)

Directions

The roots are gathered at any time of the year they can be found. Cut off the root just below the crown, wash and scrub, and dry with a towel. Slowly roast the roots in a 200° oven with the door open for 30 minutes. Watch the roots carefully to avoid burning, which will foul the taste.

Use a blender or food processor to grind the roots, but take care not to grind them too finely, especially if you'll be using a tea ball. A percolating coffee maker with a filter works the best to brew this drink. Use 1 tsp ground roots for each cup of hot water. After brewing, add 1/2 packet hot chocolate mix per cup.

Notes

This is one of best coffee substitutes that can be found. As with all coffees, it is more appealing to adults than children.

Plant:
Dandelion
pp. 80-81

Activities:
pp 129, 138

CHEESY LAMB'S QUARTERS QUICHE

Ingredients

2 cups	lamb's quarters leaves and small stems, chopped
3	eggs
1 1/2 cups	milk
1/2 cup	white flour
1 1/2 cups	mozzarella cheese, shredded
1/2 cup	butter, melted
1/2 cup	parmesan cheese
	fresh black pepper
	pinch of salt

When

Where

Directions

Mix all ingredients except the parmesan cheese and 1/2 cup of the mozzarella cheese. Whip with a fork. Grease a 9" pie pan with oil or butter and pour in the mixture. Bake in a preheated oven at 350° for 35 minutes. Remove from oven and cover the top with the extra mozzarella and parmesan cheese. Return to the oven and continue to bake for 10 minutes more. Switch to broiler for the last 2 minutes to brown the top. Watch closely to avoid burning.

Cost

UNDER
$10

Time

1
HOUR

Notes

Serves 4-6.

Plant:
Lamb's Quarters
pp. 82-83

Activity:
p. 132

PLANTAIN CHEESE PIE

When

Where

Cost

UNDER
$10

Time

1½
HOURS

Pastry ingredients

1 stick	butter, melted
3	eggs
2 cups	wheat flour
1/3 cup	milk

Sauce ingredients

4 tbsps	white flour
4 tbsps	butter
1 cup	chicken broth
1/2 cup	milk
	salt and pepper

Other ingredients

10 cups	plantain leaves, boiled
3/4 cup	mozzarella cheese, grated
1 cup	white flour for rolling dough

Directions

Pastry: In a large bowl combine wheat flour, eggs, melted butter and milk. Mix into a thick dough. Divide into 3 equal balls. Roll these balls out with a rolling pin using the white flour on a rolling surface. The finished dough should be large enough to fit inside a 9" baking dish and no thicker than 1/4".

Sauce: Melt butter in a sauce pan and whisk in white flour. Add in milk and chicken broth. While constantly whisking, bring to a boil and remove from heat. Avoid boiling for any length of time. Keep warm. Boil plantain leaves in three changes of water. Drain and squeeze out water.

Layering: Grease a 9" baking dish and place a small amount of the white sauce on the bottom, spread evenly. Place the first pastry, fitted to the shape of the dish. In order, layer: 1/2 the plantain leaves, 1/3 of the white sauce, 1/4 cup mozzarella cheese. Cover with the next pastry layer and repeat, adding the third pastry last. Top off with the last of the white sauce and mozzarella cheese. Bake covered for 35 minutes at 400°. Remove cover and broil for a few minutes to brown the top. Serves 6.

Plant:
Plantain
pp. 86-87

Activity:
p. 133

PURSLANE STUFFED TOMATOES

Ingredients

1 cup	purslane stems and leaves, washed and chopped fine
4	large tomatoes with tops and centers removed
1	small onion chopped fine
1 tbsp	olive oil
1 tsp	curry powder
1/2 clove	fresh garlic
1/2 cup	cottage cheese
1/2 cup	shredded mozzarella cheese
1/2 cup	parmesan cheese
	salt and pepper

When

Where

Cost
UNDER
$10

Directions

Sauté the onion and garlic in the olive oil. When the onion is soft add purslane, curry powder, salt and pepper. Cook over medium heat until the purslane is softened, but no longer than 5 minutes. Mix together the mozzarella and cottage cheese. Remove the purslane from the heat, add the cheeses and mix together. Fill the tomatoes with the purslane/cottage cheese mixture and cover with parmesan cheese. Bake in a covered pan for 25 minutes at 375°. Uncover and broil until the top is browned.

Time

1
HOUR

Notes

Serves 4.

Plant:
Purslane
pp. 88-89

Activity:
p. 131

ITALIAN STUFFED GRAPE LEAVES

Where

Cost
UNDER
$10

Time
1
HOUR

Plant:
Wild Grape
pp. 96–97

Activities:
pp. 122, 124

Ingredients

20-25	grape leaves (medium to large)
1 cup	instant brown rice
1	onion, chopped
1 lb	ground turkey
15 oz	canned tomato sauce
	salt and pepper
	basil
	marjoram
	mozzarella cheese, grated

Directions

Sauté the ground turkey and onions in a fry pan. Season with salt and pepper. Cook the brown rice as directed on the box. In a large sauce pan, blanch the grape leaves in salted water — 3 minutes for younger, smaller leaves and 5 minutes for larger, older leaves. Cool the leaves and dry with a towel. Cut off the stems. When the rice and ground turkey are ready, place 1 tbsp of each on the leaf and roll up as directed. Place the leaf top side down and spoon the ingredients onto the underside of the leaf. With the stem end of the leaf pointed towards yourself, fold the two sides of the leaf towards the center; then begin to roll towards the tip of the leaf. Some of the ingredients will be pushed out. Place the stuffed grape leaves in a baking dish and pour the tomato sauce over them. Season with the basil and marjoram and grate the mozzarella cheese over the top. Cover with aluminum foil and bake for 20 minutes in a preheated oven at 350°. Remove foil and brown under broiler for 3 minutes.

Serves 4 to 6.

ON THE STOVE

Teas, jellies, soups, and vegetables

- Except for teas and jellies, choose aluminum over steel or cast-iron pans; they cook faster and save energy.

- To save energy, cover your pans to shorten boiling times, but don't let them boil over.

- Turn all handles in towards the stove to avoid accidents.

- Clean the stove surface as soon as it has cooled to make it easier to remove spills.

- If using an electric stove, turn off the element in the final moments of cooking: the heat will continue to cook your food and you will save energy.

Tea Time

Brewing tea is fun and easy. Whether made from fresh or dry ingredients, wild herbal tea tends to be very mild and delicately flavored, unlike store-bought herbal or "real" teas.

When brewing with fresh ingredients, use only two teaspoons of plant material per cup. For dry ingredients, use one teaspoon. Larger quantities can be prepared using proportionally larger amounts. Steeping times will vary from plant to plant. As a general rule to avoid bitterness, never steep wild herbal teas more than five minutes.

Avoid using aluminum teapots or kettles, as they have been known to change the flavor of these more delicate teas. Similarly, soap and detergent films affect flavor: avoid teapots that have not been *thoroughly* rinsed after washing.

To make tea: Place the ingredients in a tea ball (or tea balls). Don't overstuff. For one or two cups, let the tea steep in mugs. For more than two, or for a more formal touch, pour the water over the tea ball(s) into a teapot and then allow the tea to steep.

After discovering your favorite teas, try blending several types to create new drinks. Sugar or honey can be added as sweeteners (or try brown sugar or molasses for variety).

Jelly-Making Made Easy

Jelly-making is not difficult if you follow a few basic directions. This process applies to the jelly recipes for wild rose (p. 53), wild grape (p. 52), sumac (p. 51), basswood (p. 36), and red clover (p. 47). For the purposes of this description, the harvested part of the plant will be referred to as the fruit, whether it is properly a fruit or not.

Once you have gathered the fruit, wash and rinse. Remove stems, inedible leaves, etc., and place the fruit in the refrigerator until you are ready to make the jelly.

Rendering juice, the first step, is a simple process that involves boiling the fruit; in a large stainless steel or glass sauce pan, combine the fruit and water, cover and bring to a boil over a medium-high heat. Let boil briskly for 10-20 minutes, depending on the recipe.

While the juice is being rendered, sterilize the jars and lids by boiling them for ten minutes in a large pot of water. When you remove the jars and lids from the water, do not touch the insides, and place them on a clean surface. Do not remove them too soon; they should cool only slightly before filling.

Next, strain the juice into a bowl, using a sieve or cheese cloth. A colander may be used if it has very small holes or if it is lined with cheese cloth. After the juice has been strained, gather the ends of the cheese cloth and twist to squeeze out any juice remaining in the pulp. This will cloud the juice but yield more flavor and jelly.

Next, measure the juice, returning it to the now-empty saucepan.

Be especially sure to avoid burning the mixture from now on. Bring to a boil over medium heat. Just as the juice comes to a boil, add the pectin in the indicated amount. After adding the pectin, stir until the juice begins to boil again. Stirring constantly, add sugar in an amount equal to the juice you measured (i.e. if you measured out 3 cups of juice, you add 3 cups of sugar). Add sugar one cup at a time, and let that cup dissolve completely before adding the next.

Still stirring, return to a boil, reduce the heat slightly and let boil for 1-2 minutes. Remove from heat and skim.

Pour the jelly into jars and seal. Use a funnel when filling the jars—spilling onto the lip of the jar will cause a bad seal and allow the jelly to spoil unless it is kept refrigerated. Sealed, the unopened jars can be stored at room temperature for several years without spoiling.

The jelly purist will tell you that using store-bought pectin isn't as authentic, but until you're experienced, it's best to stick to pre-made pectin to ensure a successful jelly. Pectin is a natural component of fruits, a long molecule that becomes swollen with water when in the jelly broth. In the hot water, the molecules twist themselves around and around, so that when the jelly cools, they become entangled like a twiggy thicket. It is these interlocking molecules that make the jelly firm. Too much water, sugar or acid inhibits this entanglement. Since the amount of pectin found in fruits is highly variable, it is much easier to use store-bought pectin to achieve jelling.

Testing to see if the boiling mixture will jell is relatively easy. Chill a small plate or dish in the refrigerator and as the jelly mixture is on its final boil, drop a teaspoon or so of the mixture onto the dish. Within a minute or so it should jell. If it doesn't, boil off a little more water or add a little more pectin and try again.

SWEET BASSWOOD JELLY

Ingredients

3 cups	fresh basswood flowers, packed
1 1/2 cups	water
1 cup	sugar
1 package	pectin

Directions

Using cold water, wash the flowers free of any debris or bugs. Place in a sauce pan along with the 1 1/2 cups of water. Bring to a boil while crushing flowers with a large wooden spoon. Simmer for 10-15 minutes, covered. Remove from heat and strain through a colander lined with cheese cloth. Measure this strained juice and return to heat. Squeeze out any extra juice. Bring to a boil and add an amount of sugar equal to the juice you measured. Return to a boil and add the pectin. Continue to boil while constantly stirring. Boil hard for two minutes while stirring and test for jelling by placing a drop on a cool plate. Pour into sterilized jars and seal.

Notes

See pp. 34-35 for additional jelly-making tips.

Makes 16 to 24 oz.

Plant:
Basswood
pp. 74-75

Activities:
*pp. 127, 135,
140*

MORNING BASSWOOD BREW

Ingredients (per cup)

2-3	fresh basswood flowers *or*
3-6	dry flowers
	water

Directions

Boil as much water as you need. For one cup, place the ingredients in a tea ball, place the tea ball in your mug, and pour the water over it. Steep for 2 to 3 minutes until the tea is light green to yellow with a sweet aroma. For larger amounts of tea, use three small tea balls or one large one in a teapot. Don't over-pack the tea ball; the hot water needs to flow in and around the flowers that are inside.

Notes

See pp. 33-34 for more tea-making hints.

Plant:
Basswood
pp. 74-75

Activities:
pp. 127, 140

CATTAIL
"CORN" ON THE COB

When

Where

Cost

UNDER
$5

Time

15
MINS.

Ingredients

10-12	cattail flower tops (cobs)
	butter
	salt
	water

Directions

Bring a large pot of water to a boil and add the cattail cobs. Boil for 5 minutes and remove from the heat and allow to stand for another 5 to 10 minutes. Drain the water and brush with butter and salt to taste. Eat like corn on the cob. Center stalk is not edible.

Notes

Serves 4.

KIDS' CHOICE:
CATTAILS AND CHEESE

Ingredients

25	cattail stalks, peeled and sliced white centers
	pot of water
1 cup	cheddar cheese, shredded
2 tbsp	butter

Cheese sauce:

1 tbsp	butter
1 tbsp	white flour
1 cup	chicken broth (1 bouillon cube)
1 1/2 cups	shredded cheddar cheese
	fresh ground pepper

When

Where

Cost
UNDER
$5

Time
30 MINS.

Directions

Boil the stalks until tender, but no longer than 10 minutes. Remove from the water and place in an oven-proof dish. Add butter and cheese on top and put under broiler to melt. You must watch closely to avoid burning.

Or: In a small sauce pan melt the butter. Whisk in the flour until smooth using low heat. Dissolve one bouillon cube in one cup of boiling water. Add this chicken broth to the flour mixture and continue whisking. Turn up the heat to medium high and when the mixture is smooth add the shredded cheese. Continue to whisk and bring to a boil. Remove from heat and pour over the boiled shoots. Top off with fresh black pepper.

*Plant:
Cattail
pp. 76-77*

Notes

Serves 2. Recipe can be doubled.

*Activity:
pp. 129, 146*

LEMON BUTTERED CURLED DOCK

When

Where

Cost
UNDER $5

Time
30 MINS.

Ingredients

10-12	curled dock leaves
	pot of water
1/3 cup	chicken broth (1/2 bouillon cube)
1/4 cup	lemon juice
4-8 tbsp	softened butter
	black pepper

(Lime juice can also be used along with the lemon to make a lemon/lime sauce. Use lime to lemon in a ratio of 1:3.)

Directions

Blanch the leaves in 3-4 changes of boiling water (do not steam the leaves). In a sauce pan boil the chicken broth and lemon juice together. Reduce this down to 1/3 cup. Remove from the heat and while still hot, drop the butter, one tbsp at a time, into the hot sauce. Whisk or whip until the butter is melted. Continue dropping butter and whisking until smooth. Pour the sauce over the blanched leaves and serve hot with a dusting of pepper.

Notes

Serves 2. Recipe can be doubled.

Plant:
Curled Dock
pp. 78-79

Activities:
pp. 124, 127,
138

HEARTY CURLED DOCK SOUP

Ingredients

30	small (about 6") curled dock leaves or
15	large (about 12") curled dock leaves
3	medium potatoes, chopped
1	medium onion, chopped
1 clove	garlic, chopped fine
1 tbsp	butter
3 cups	chicken broth or water
	black pepper

When

Where

Directions

Sauté onions, garlic and potatoes in butter over medium heat. When these are soft, add chicken stock and dock leaves. Bring to a boil, cover, and reduce to a simmer for 20-30 minutes. Cool the soup and puree in a blender or food processor. Add pepper to taste.

Cost

UNDER
$10

Time

1
HOUR

Notes

This is an excellent soup that doesn't need to be seasoned if chicken stock is used instead of water.

Plant:
Curled Dock
pp. 78-79

Activities:
pp. 124, 127,
138

SOUTH OF THE BORDER DANDELIONS

We know that many people wish their dandelions were south of the border, but this recipe may make you change your mind.

When

Where

Cost
UNDER
$5

Time
30
MINS.

Ingredients

2 cups	dandelion crowns, washed
12 oz	Mexican salsa (mild or hot)
	Pot of water

Directions

Peel the outer layers off the crowns and wash off any remaining dirt. Blanch the crowns in two changes of salted water. Drain. Mix in the salsa. Serve hot.

Notes

The small unopened "buds" found by pushing back the larger outer leaves can also be used in this recipe. The white crown is the part of the plant found beneath the soil level, between the leaves and above the brown tap root. It is often 1" long. Cut off the leaves and discard. Remove the root and save for roasting. Use only the white crowns and be sure to remove the outer layers before washing. Most of the time the crowns are good enough to eat raw but sample a small amount first.

Serves 2.

Plant:
Dandelion
pp. 80-81

Activities:
pp. 129, 138

LAMB'S QUARTERS IN MUSTARD SAUCE

Ingredients

5 cups	lamb's quarters leaves and small stems
1/4 cup	dry mustard
2 tsp	oil
1/2 tsp	salt
1/4 cup	water

When

Where

Directions

Steam the lamb's quarters until tender, approximately 10 minutes. Set aside. Mix dry mustard, oil and salt together. Boil the water and add to mustard while stirring until smooth. Pour mustard over the steamed lamb's quarters or use as a dip.

Cost

UNDER
$5

Notes

Makes about 1/3 cup of sauce (serves 2). Recipe can be doubled.

Time

30
MINS.

Plant:
Lamb's Quarters
pp. 82-83

Activities:
pp. 132, 144

LAMB'S QUARTERS
SIDE DISH

Ingredients

5 cups	lamb's quarters leaves and small stems
2 tbsps	butter
2 tbsps	white flour
1/4 tsp	fresh black pepper
1 cup	chicken broth (instant bouillon)
1 clove	garlic minced
1 tsp	basil
1 tsp	chives
1 tsp	oregano

Directions

In a sauce pan melt butter and saute minced garlic. Whisk in the flour until smooth. Add the pepper, basil, chives, oregano and chicken broth. Cook while whisking until thick, about 3 minutes. Avoid boiling. Steam the lamb's quarters. Don't overcook. While still hot, serve the lamb's quarters with the sauce over the top.

Notes

Lamb's quarters can be gathered when only a few inches tall or when it has grown to several feet and has flowers blooming. Either way, this plant doesn't become bitter. Avoid the large stems for their obvious toughness.

Serves 2-4.

*Plant:
Lamb's
Quarters
pp. 82-83*

*Activities:
pp. 132, 144*

CHEDDAR CHEESE PLANTAIN

Ingredients

5 cups	young plantain leaves
	water

Cheese sauce:

1 tbsp	butter
1 tbsp	white flour
1 cup	chicken broth (1 bouillon cube)
1 1/2 cups	shredded cheddar cheese
	fresh ground pepper

Directions

Boil the plantain leaves. One change of water should be all that is needed if the leaves are young enough. Older, tougher leaves should be boiled in several changes of water. Transferring the leaves back and forth between two pots of water will speed up the process.

Cheese sauce: In a small sauce pan melt the butter. Whisk in the flour until smooth using a low heat, then set aside. Dissolve one bouillon cube in one cup of boiling water. Add the chicken broth and continue whisking. Turn up the heat to medium high and when the mixture is smooth, add the shredded cheese. Continue to whisk and bring to a boil.

Remove from the heat and pour over the cooked plantain leaves. Dust with fresh ground black pepper.

Plant:
Plantain
pp. 86-87

Activities:
pp. 133, 144

Notes

Serves 2.

RED CLOVER TEA ROYALE

When

Where

Cost
UNDER
$2

Time
15
MINS.

Fresh ingredients per cup

3-5   fresh red clover flowers
           water

Dry ingredients per cup

5-7   dry red clover flowers
           water

Directions

Gather the flowers any time you find them blooming. To dry, lay the flowers on a window screen in a cool dry place. Flowers can also be dried in a food dehydrator (see p. 142).

Boil the water and remove from the heat. Put the flowers in one or several tea balls depending on how much tea you want to make. Steep for 5 minutes. A stronger tea can be made by allowing the flowers to steep up to 10 minutes.

Notes

See more tips on tea-making, p. 33.

Plant:
Red Clover
pp. 90-91

Activities:
pp. 131, 138

SWEET-TOOTH
SWEET CLOVER JELLY

Ingredients

2 cups	red clover flowers, tightly packed
1 1/2 cups	water
1 cup	sugar
1 packet	fruit pectin

Directions

In a medium sauce pan, place the flowers in the water. Boil while crunching the flowers with a wooden spoon. Continue boiling for 5 to 10 minutes until all the flowers lose their red color and start to fall apart. Strain out all of the flowers by pouring through a cheese cloth or a colander with very small holes. Be sure to extract out all of the juice by crushing and squeezing. Return the juice to the stove, start boiling and add the pectin. Bring to a boil again and add sugar. Return to a boil and allow to boil for 1 to 2 minutes, stirring constantly. Pour into sterile jars.

Notes

Makes 12 to 16 oz. Jelly recipes cannot be doubled. See jelly-making tips, pp. 34-35.

When

Where

Cost

UNDER
$5

Time

1
HOUR

Plant:
Red Clover
pp. 90-91

Activities:
pp. 132, 135

FRESH NETTLE FETTUCINE

When

Where

Cost
UNDER
$10

Time
1
HOUR

Plant:
Stinging
Nettles
pp. 92-93

Activity:
p. 129

Ingredients

2 cups	fresh nettle tops (top 2-3" of plant), washed
1/2 stick	butter
10 small	
or 5 large	mushrooms
1	shallot, minced (can use onion)
1 tbsp	olive oil
1/2 lb	fettuccine or linguini pasta noodles
	fresh black pepper

Sauce

2 tbsp	butter
2 tbsp	white flour
1/4 tsp	salt
1 cup	chicken broth

Directions

Cook pasta as directed on the box. Blanch the nettles in boiling water. Drain and rinse nettles, set aside. Sauté the shallots or onions and mushrooms in olive oil. Keep warm and set aside.

Sauce: Melt butter in sauce pan. Stir in flour and mix well. Add chicken broth and salt and cook over medium heat until thick. Avoid boiling. Top the pasta with the nettles and mushrooms. Pour white sauce over entire dish. Dust with black pepper.

Notes

Serves 4.

LEMON GARLIC NETTLE TOPS

Ingredients

3 cups	nettle tops (top 2-3" of plant), washed
	pot of water
1/3 cup	chicken broth, 1/2 bouillon cube
1/4 cup	lemon juice
2 tbsps	shallots or onion, finely chopped
1 sm. clove	garlic, finely chopped
4-8 tbsps	softened butter
	black pepper

Directions

Always wear gloves when collecting nettles. Wash the nettles with cold water and chop coarsely. Boil the tops for 5 minutes and drain the water. Boil together the lemon juice and chicken broth, stirring in the shallots, garlic and several shakes of black pepper. Reduce down to 1/3 cup and remove from heat. Strain out the shallots, garlic and pepper. While still hot, drop the butter, 1 tbsp at a time, into the sauce and whisk or whip until smooth. Pour the sauce over the hot cooked nettles.

When

Where

Cost
UNDER
$5

Time

1
HOUR

Plant:
Stinging
Nettles
pp. 92-93

Activity:
p. 129

ONION GARLIC NETTLE SOUP

When

Where

Cost

UNDER
$ 5

Time

1
HOUR

Ingredients

40	nettles tops (top 2-3" of plant), washed
1	large onion
1 clove	garlic
3	large potatoes, chopped
4 cups	chicken stock
	olive oil
	salt and pepper

Directions

Always wear gloves when gathering nettles. In a large sauce pan, sauté the onion, potato and garlic in the olive oil. When the onion and potato are soft, add the chicken stock and the washed nettle tops. Cover and boil the mixture for 15 minutes until the potatoes are well cooked. Allow to cool, then pour soup into a blender or food processor and purée (liquefy). Return to pan and add salt and pepper to taste.

Notes

Serves 4. Recipe can be doubled.

Plant:
Stinging
Nettles
pp. 92-93

Activity:
p. 129

LATE SUMMER SUMAC JELLY

Ingredients

1 cup	sumac fruits (seeds)
2 cups	water
1 package	pectin
2 cups	sugar

Directions

Break the clusters of seeds into a sauce pan and add the water. Boil for up to 5 minutes. Strain through a cheese cloth to remove fine particles. Return to a boil and add the pectin. Bring back to a boil and add sugar and return to boil for 1-2 minutes while constantly stirring. Skim. Pour into sterile jars.

Sumac syrup is made by omitting the pectin from the above recipe. Syrup can be used on ice cream, pancakes and even chicken (see p. 20).

Notes

Makes 28-30 oz. Jelly recipes *cannot* be doubled. See jelly-making tips pp. 34-35.

When

Where

Cost

Time

Plant:
Sumac
pp. 94-95

Activities:
pp. 127, 135

WILD GRAPE JELLY

When

Where

Cost
UNDER
$5

Time
1
HOUR

Ingredients

2 cups	grapes, washed and removed from the stem
1 cup	water
1-2 cups	sugar
1 package	fruit pectin

Directions

Wash and remove the stems from the grapes. Some of the unripe green grapes can be used to add extra pectin and flavor. Simmer the grapes over medium-low heat, covered for 10 minutes. Crushing the grapes helps to release the juice. Strain the juice through several layers of cheese cloth or a colander lined with cheese cloth. Measure this juice to determine how much sugar is needed. Return the juice to the stove and bring to a boil over medium heat. Add the pectin and return to a boil. Add an amount of sugar equal to the amount of juice you just measured. Bring back to a boil for 1-2 minuites. Skim and pour.

Notes

Some varieties of wild grape have enough natural pectin in them to produce jelly, but the pectin level varies widely among varieties. Adding extra pectin will ensure you don't end up with grape juice.

Makes 16 oz to 20 oz. Jelly recipes cannot be doubled.

See pp. 34-35 for more jelly-making tips.

Plant:
Wild Grape
pp. 96-97

Activities:
pp. 122, 127,
135

WILD & HIP JELLY

Ingredients

2 cups	rose hips, washed
2 cups	water
2 cups	sugar
1 package	fruit pectin

When

Directions

Start the water boiling and add the hips. Crush while boiling for 15-20 minutes. Strain the juice through a cheese cloth into a clean pan, be sure to squeeze out every drop. Return to the heat, boil and add the pectin. Add sugar and again return to a boil for 1-2 minutes while constantly stirring. Pour into a sterile jar and cover.

Where

Notes

Makes 28-30 oz. Jelly recipes cannot be doubled.

See jelly-making tips, pp. 34-35.

Cost
UNDER
$10

Time
1
HOUR

Plant:
Wild Rose
pp. 98-99

Activity:
pp. 126, 135

WILD ROSE MEDLEY TEA

Where

Cost

UNDER
$ 2

Time

15
MINS

Ingredients

| 4-5 | fresh young rose leaves and petals |
| 1 cup | hot water |

or

| 12-15 | rose leaves and petals |
| 1 pot | hot water |

In late summer, rose hips can be added in just about any amount for extra flavor and vitamin C.

Directions

Boil water and remove from the stove. Steep the rose leaves and hips in the hot water by using a tea ball or bag. The longer you steep it, the stronger the flavor. Don't over-steep because it may turn bitter.

Notes

See pp. 33-34 for more tea-making hints.

Plant:
Wild Rose
pp. 98-99

Activities:
pp. 126, 144

LEMON BUTTERED WINTERCRESS

Ingredients

8-10	winter cress flower tops
1/2	fresh lemon
or 1 tsp	concentrated lemon juice
	water
2 tbsps	butter
1 tsp	dill weed, chopped fine
	salt and pepper

When

Directions

Bring water to a boil and add the flower tops. Boil for 3 minutes and remove. Start a fresh pot of water boiling and add the tops. Repeat once more for a total of three changes of water, boiling for 3 minutes each time. Melt butter in a small sauce pan and whisk in the lemon and dill. Butter should appear milky. Drain the flower tops and cover with the sauce. Salt and pepper to taste.

Where

Cost

UNDER $5

Time

30 MINS.

Notes

Serves 2.

Plant:
Winter Cress
pp. 100-101

Activities:
pp. 129, 144

LEMON WOOD SORREL FISH SAUCE

Ingredients

1 cup	wood sorrel stems, leaves, and flowers
1/3 cup	chicken broth (1/2 cup bouillon cube)
1/4 cup	lemon juice
2 tbsps	finely chopped shallots or onion
1 small	clove garlic finely chopped
	black pepper
4-8 tbsps	softened butter
2 fillets	your favorite fish

Directions

Wash and finely chop the wood sorrel stems, leaves and flowers. Boil together the chicken broth, lemon juice, shallots, garlic and black pepper. Reduce down to 1/3 cup and strain out the shallot, garlic and pepper. Remove from the heat. While still hot, drop the butter, one tbsp at a time into the sauce and whisk or whip until smooth. Add the chopped wood sorrel and mix thoroughly. Pour hot over steamed or broiled fish.

Notes

Serves 4.

Cost
UNDER
$15

Time
1
HOUR

Plant:
*Yellow Wood
Sorrel*
pp. 102-103

Activities:
pp. 129, 144

NO COOKING REQUIRED

Salads and Trail Nibbles

Use the pickling recipes when you can prepare them on one occasion and taste them on another.

The following Plantworks plants are great just freshly picked.

cattail .... stalk
basswood .... young leaves
plantain .... leaves
purslane .... leaves and stems
wild grape .... tendrils
wild rose .... hips and petals
yellow wood sorrel .. leaves and fruits.

Unless you know for sure the area you are harvesting has *not* been sprayed with herbicides or pesticides, assume that it has and wash your harvest thoroughly before eating.

Make sure to obey park restrictions on picking, or ask for special permission for your group to pick a given amount of a plant at a designated time.

Remember to nibble, not gorge; these plants will be new to your system.

When

Where

Cost
UNDER
$5

Time
15
MINS.

FOREST-FRESH BASSWOOD SALAD

Ingredients

5 cups	basswood leaves
4 slices	bacon, fried and crumbled
1/2	small onion, sliced
5	radishes, sliced
	dressing of choice (creamy style)
	black pepper to taste

Directions

Wash the radishes, onion and basswood leaves in cold water. Pat dry with a towel. Let bacon cool before crumbling. Mix all ingredients in a large bowl and serve with dressing and black pepper.

Notes

Serves 4.

Plant:
Basswood
pp. 74-75

Activities:
pp. 122, 124,
127, 140

CHOPPED 'N' PICKLED CATTAILS

Ingredients

20-30	cattail stalks, washed
1/2	large onion chopped
1 clove	garlic chopped
	salt and pepper to taste
1/4 cup	vegetable oil
1/2 cup	red wine vinegar
	several 12 oz glass jars

Directions

Cut shoots to fit in glass jars. Add shoots to jar until full. Whisk oil and vinegar together. Add onion, garlic, salt and pepper. Pour this marinade over the shoots to fill the jar. Seal and refrigerate overnight. Serve with salad, snack right out of the jar, or serve as an appetizer.

When

Where

Cost

UNDER $5

Time

+ overnight wait

15 MINS.

Plant:
Cattail
pp. 76-77

Activities:
pp. 129, 146

DIP INTO CATTAILS

When

Where

Cost
UNDER
$5

Time
15
MINS.

Ingredients

20-30	cattail stalks, washed
8 oz	sour cream
1 package	dry onion soup mix
	crackers of your choice (optional)

Directions

Mix dry onion soup mix into sour cream. Cut shoots to 3 to 4 inches and serve with chip dip and crackers. A great introduction for people new to wild edibles.

Plant:
Cattail
pp. 76-77

Activities:
pp. 129, 146

LAMB'S QUARTERS SESAME SUMMER SALAD

Ingredients

2 cups	lamb's quarters leaves, small stems
1	green pepper, sliced
1/2 head	lettuce
1	cucumber, sliced
1	large tomato, sliced
	sesame seeds (salted or unsalted)
	ranch dressing

Directions

Wash the lamb's quarters and chop into salad size pieces. Wash and chop the lettuce in the same way. Slice the tomato, cucumber and pepper. Toss all of the ingredients together. Top with dressing and sesame seeds.

Notes

Serves 2-4.

When

Where

Cost

UNDER $5

Time

15 MINS.

Plant:
Lamb's
Quarters
pp. 82-83

Activities:
pp. 132, 144

PLANTAIN DELIGHT

Ingredients

5 cups	young plantain leaves, chopped
1	large tomato, sliced
1	large avocado, sliced
4 tbsps	red wine vinegar
2 tbsps	oil
1 tsp	sugar
1 pinch	basil
	black pepper to taste

Where

Directions

Toss the washed plantain leaves, tomato and avocado together. Combine red wine vinegar, oil, sugar and basil in a small container and shake until the sugar is dissolved. Pour over salad and season with freshly ground black pepper.

Notes

Serves 4.

Plant:
Plantain
pp. 86-87

Activities:
pp. 133, 144

VANILLA YOGURT PURSLANE SUPREME

Ingredients

1 cup	purslane, washed and chopped
8 oz.	vanilla yogurt
1/2	medium cucumber, peeled and cubed
1/4 cup	unsalted sesame seeds

Directions

Mix all the ingredients in large bowl and chill.

Notes

This makes a great light lunch. You can use any flavor (or unflavored) yogurt. This is especially useful as a side dish with hot foods.

Serves 2.

When

Where

Cost

UNDER
$5

Time

15
MINS.

Plant:
Purslane
pp. 88-89

Activity:
p. 131

PURSLANE PEPPERONI SALAD

Ingredients

2 cups	purslane leaves and stems, washed and chopped
1 cup	lettuce, washed and cut (can be omitted)
1/2 cup	pepperoni cut to bite size (3 oz)
1/4 cup	monterey jack cheese cut to bite size (2 oz)
5	mild salad peppers

3 tbsps	red wine vinegar
2 tbsps	oil
	salt and pepper to taste

Directions

Dressing: Mix together the oil, vinegar, salt and pepper and whisk until smooth.

Toss the remaining ingredients together and serve with this dressing or use your own favorite.

Notes

Serves 4. You can double this recipe.

Plant:
Purslane
pp. 88-89

Activity:
p. 131

DAD'S PICKLED PURSLANE

Ingredients

2 cups	purslane stems and leaves, washed
1/4 cup	onion, finely chopped
1/2 clove	garlic, finely chopped
2 tsps	sugar
1/4 tsp	salt
	black pepper
	white distilled vinegar

When

Where

Directions

Cut purslane to fit 12 oz jar. Fill jar 3/4 full with the purslane. Add the onion, garlic, salt, sugar and several grindings of fresh black pepper. Fill jar to the top with white distilled vinegar. Cover tightly and shake well. Let stand at room temperature for 2 hours, then refrigerate.

Cost

UNDER $5

Time

30 MINS.

Notes

More purslane can be added to this mixture as it is eaten to provide a continuous supply.

Plant:
Purslane
pp. 88-89

Activity:
p. 131

SUMAC SUMMER REFRESHER

When

Where

Cost

UNDER
$ 5

Time

1
HOUR

Ingredients

4 to 6	large clusters of red sumac fruits (seeds)
1 pitcher	cold water
	sugar

Directions

Taste the sumac fruits for tartness. Use only tart fruits. Soak the berries in cold water for 15-30 minutes while crushing and breaking up the clusters. Strain through a cheese cloth and sweeten to your taste.

Notes

Fruits can be harvested in winter.

Plant:
Sumac
pp. 94-95

Activities:
pp. 127, 138

BACON POTATO SALAD

Ingredients

2 cups	small, young grape leaves and tendrils
1/2 head	lettuce, chopped
2	large potatoes, cubed
5 strips	bacon
	ranch dressing

When

Directions

Boil the cubed potatoes until soft. Fry the bacon until crisp. Cool potatoes with cold water and crumble bacon. Wash grape leaves and tendrils and mix with lettuce. Mix in potatoes and bacon. Chill and serve as a cool summer salad with ranch dressing.

Where

Cost
UNDER
$5

Notes

There is cooking involved in this recipe, but the plant itself is not cooked.

Serves 2-4.

Time
45
MINS.

Plant:
Wild Grape
pp. 96-97

Activities:
pp. 122, 124,
127

ROSE PETAL CANDY

When

Where

Cost

UNDER
$5

Time

45
MINS.

Ingredients

12-24	wild rose flower petals
2-3	egg whites
1/2 cup	sugar

Directions

Wash the petals, being careful not to bruise or tear them. Separate the eggs. Brush or dip the petals with a slightly beaten egg white. Sprinkle with sugar and dry in a food dehydrator (see activity, p. 142 and discussion of plant drying, p. 9). Do not over-dry; the petals are done when they are still flexible. They can also be left out overnight to dry.

Notes

Gather only a few petals to add color and taste to a fresh salad. Rose petals can be refreshing to eat right off the plant when you are out hiking. Eight to ten petals can be added to a hot glass of water for a great-tasting tea.

Plant:
Wild Rose
pp. 98-99

Activities:
pp. 126, 144

CRISP WINTER CRESS SALAD

Ingredients

2 cups	winter cress leaves, very young, washed
2 cups	lettuce, washed and cut
1 cup	sharp cheddar cheese, cubed or shredded
1/4 cup	sesame seeds
	parmesan cheese
	black pepper
	ranch dressing

When

Where

Directions

Toss winter cress and lettuce together. Add cheese and sesame seeds. Sprinkle with parmesan and several grindings of black pepper.

Cost
UNDER
$5

Time
15
MINS.

Notes

Serves 4.

Plant:
Winter Cress
pp. 100-101

Activities:
pp. 138, 144

B.C.T. SANDWICH (BACON, CRESS, TOMATO)

When

Where

Cost

UNDER
$5

Time

30
MINS.

Ingredients

10-20	winter cress leaves
6-8 strips	bacon
	mayonnaise
4 slices	bread

Directions

Wash the winter cress leaves in cold water. Toast the bread. Fry the bacon until crisp. Use winter cress leaves in place of lettuce in this classic B.L.T.—or in any of your other favorite sandwiches!

Notes

Serves 2.

Plant:
Winter Cress
pp. 100-101

Activities:
pp. 138, 144

NATURAL HISTORIES

This natural history section is designed to give you all the information you'll need to successfully locate each Plantworks plant. If you are at all in doubt about a plant's identity, please refer to an additional guide (see bibliography, pp. 151-152) or consult a naturalist at your local nature center.

Be sure to follow rule number 1 of the Golden Rules of Harvesting Wild Plants (see pp. 4-5) and never proceed unless you are 110% sure you have located the right plant !

The language of botanical names, created by the Swedish botanist Carolus Linnaeus, is universally accepted as the official scientific naming system of plants and animals. The Latin name is always in two parts, the genus (grouping of related species) name first and the species (specific plant) name second. The Latin names for many plant families end in the suffix "*aceae*", which is pronounced "a-see-ee". The trick is to pronounce every letter in each Latin name.

The meaning of the Latin plant names for these and other plants can provide clues to the plants' identities. The species name "*crispus*", for example, is Latin for crisped or curled and refers to the curled edges of the dock plant's leaves.

PLANTWORKS
PLANT FACTS

Green plants are the foundation of life itself. They alone fix energy from the sun. From humans at the top of the food chain to simpler creatures further down, all animal life is dependent on plants. Without the food, energy and oxygen green plants produce as by-products, there would be no life on planet Earth.

- There are 380,000 different kinds of plants.

- 400 plant species are lost each year to extinction.

- 40-50% of all medicinal drugs originate in wild plants.

- 1/4 of these medicinal drugs come from the rain forest.

- Only 1% of all plants have been screened for potential medicinal drug sources.

- It is estimated that 2,000 rain forest plants could have cancer-fighting effects.

- 90% of the world's food comes from 20 individual plant species.

- 1/2 of the world's food comes from 3 plant species: corn, wheat and rice.

- Plants have the exclusive ability to convert the energy of sunlight to chemical energy using the pigment chlorophyll; plants are the primary producers of all food on Earth.

- 1/2 of all plant species are found in the tropics, but 400 square miles of the Amazon forest are lost per year.

- Rice varieties, which are species of grass, feed half of the world's population.

- Only 2% of all farm output is organically grown.

- 1/4 of all fruits and vegetables in the U. S. are grown in California.

- More than enough grain is grown each year in the world to feed all humans.

- In the U.S., 90% of the grain harvested is now fed to animals, making the use of land in the U.S. much less efficient than in China. Foods considered necessary to feed 200 million in the west would feed 1500 million Chinese.

The food pyramid

AMERICAN BASSWOOD

Tilia americana   The Linden Family: *Tiliaceae*

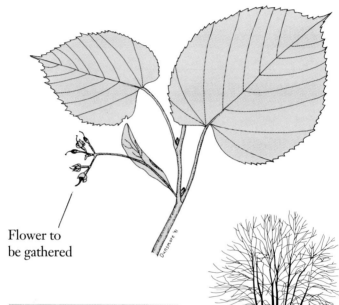

Flower to
be gathered

Above: Winter silhouette. Note
multiple trunks.

Below: Immature leaf

*Recipes:
pp. 36, 37,
58*

If you have access to a woodland, you should be able to locate a basswood tree easily. The young leaves and aromatic flowers of the American basswood or linden tree provide excellent trail snacks and are edible in salads and teas. The young leaves are ready for harvest in the spring for use in salad and the flowers can be harvested in summer to make tea. Two tablespoons of fresh flowers make one cup of tea. There is no caffeine in this refreshing "tree-bel-tea" which is especially appealing to young people when it is iced.

If you find a multi-trunked (tilling) tree you have probably located a basswood. Young trees have smooth light gray bark which darkens and develops deep vertical grooves as the tree ages. A key identification feature of the basswood is its heart-shaped large leaf (4-6 in) with sharply serrated edges. The leaves are asymmetrical—that is, the midrib of the leaf doesn't divide it into two equal parts.

The basswood's large, creamy, off-white flowers hang down from long stalks. In the spring you can find flowering basswoods with your nose; their fragrance can be detected up to 1/4 mile away if the wind is in your favor. You may need a ladder to reach some of its flowers because this tree reaches heights of 60-80 feet.

Reaching flowers on this tall tree is no problem for the honey bee, though. Nicknamed the "Bee Tree," the basswood seems to hum in early summer as hundreds of these pollinators collect pollen and nectar from the basswood's fragrant flowers. The honey made from basswood flowers is strongly flavored, but very popular. Pollinated flowers produce a crop of winged seeds every year.

The basswood is a very common tree throughout the eastern United States. Two species besides *Tilia americana* are found in some areas. Because it is fast-growing and long-lived, it is often chosen as a tree to line city streets and parks. Native Americans have used the bark of basswood to make baskets and twine, a time-consuming and difficult task, but one rewarded by extremely light and durable products. The light-colored wood of the basswood is used for furniture, musical instruments and yardsticks. It is also a choice wood for wood carvers .

CATTAIL

Typha spp.   The Cattail Family: *Typhaceae*

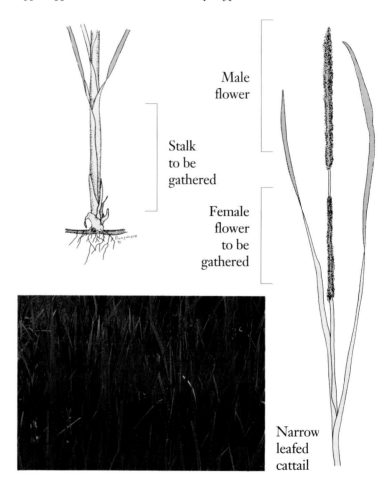

Male
flower

Stalk
to be
gathered

Female
flower
to be
gathered

Narrow
leafed
cattail

*Recipes:
pp. 16, 38,
39, 59, 60*

This plant is probably the star of the plant world, and certainly of the wetlands habitat. It is prominent, easily identified and valuable to many forms of wildlife as a food and fiber source. Both the common (*Typha latfolia*) and narrow-leaved (*Typha angustifolia*) species qualify as good sources of wild edibles for humans, too. In addition to the leaf width, the two species are also distinguished in that the common cattail does not have a space between the male and female flowers.

Look for this tall slender-leaved plant in marshy areas. Dense 3-to-9-foot tall stands line shallow pond edges. To protect your feet (and footwear), wear rubber boots when going out to harvest it. The white inner parts of the stalks are the part you'll want to eat, so a pocket knife is useful to cut away the green outer layers of the stalk and to slice the white inner parts into pieces to eat. The stalks are edible in the spring and early summer, but they get rather stringy as the weather gets hotter.

The brown cigar-like part of the cattail, seen later in fall, is the portion of the plant which gives it its common name. This brown section (often used in dried flower arrangements) is actually a compact structure of its female flowers. In early summer, it is green and pencil-thick, and ready to harvest for cooking and eating (see "Cattail Corn on the Cob," p. 38). During cooking, you'll enjoy the familiar sweet corn smell.

Each year the exact timing (phenology) of edible plant parts varies due to weather conditions. You can see when cattails are at the proper stage for "Corn on the Cob" by watching roadside ditches as you drive by. The more you harvest these and other Plantworks plants, the more you fine-tune your observational skills, and the more success you'll have each year in timing your harvest.

The cattail is a major plant of the wetland areas. Cattail—and wetlands in general—provide vital shelter, food and nesting habitat for animals such as ducks, geese, turtles, muskrats, beavers, and red-winged and yellow-headed blackbirds. Just for the variety, these cattail hunts may become your favorite hike. Taking students through the marsh can be an eye-opening experience. Try to list all of the birds, turtles and even mammals that you encounter!

The Ojibwa people used the dried reed-like leaves for weaving into mats that lined their wigwams. They moved these lightweight, sheltering mats from their maple syruping sites to their wild-ricing and fishing villages. (see p. 146 to make mats)

CURLED (CURLY) DOCK:

Rumex crispus   The Smartweed Family: *Polygonaceae*

seed

curled
dock in
winter

in
early
spring

in mid-
summer

note curled-
edged leaves

*Recipes:
pp. 26, 27,
40, 41*

detail of flowers
in summer

You probably have seen curled dock, a member of the Smartweed family (*Polygonaceae*), hundreds of times without realizing that both its leaves and ripened seeds are choice edibles. Many different kinds of dock grow throughout the continental United States and all are safe to eat. In different parts of the country it may be known as "Yellow Dock" or "Sour Dock."

We like to call this a 55-mile-per-hour plant because it is easy to identify from car windows, in open fields and along roadsides. In the early spring, look for last year's stalks. The new green plants, about 12-18 inches high, whose leaves are edible, will be near the old 3-6 foot brown stalks.

The curled dock leaves are distinctively curly and grow in a circular array at the plant's base and along the stem. When the large main rib or vein of each leaf becomes red with age, the leaf is too bitter to be eaten raw. It's still fine for cooking, if you remember to change the water twice. This is a biennial plant; it takes two years to reach its flowering stage.

In late summer the greenish spires of tiny curled dock flowers turn to dark-brown triangular-shaped seeds. In the fall, look for brown seed clusters on top of tall brown stalks. The seeds can be stripped from the stalk by hand and stored in a glass jar. Try to pick seeds after several sunny days so that they are not wet and subject to mold. Check for and wash away any insects that may also be enjoying this plant. Grind the seeds in a blender to form a refined flour which may be added to muffins and sweet bread recipes. It is a heavy flour and should always be used in combination with white or wheat flour.

Curled dock is high in fiber and has more vitamin A in its leaves than an equal amount of carrots: 12,900 I.U. of Vitamin A for a 100 gram portion. This portion also contains 2 grams of protein, 119 milligrams of vitamin C, and only 28 calories. The ground seeds have a similar flavor to that of curled dock's relative, buckwheat. The tangy flavor of the young leaves, harvested in spring, are great in soups or as a cooked vegetable. Historically, curled dock root has been used for pharmaceutical purposes as an astringent and laxative.

COMMON DANDELION

Taraxacum officinale   The Composite Family: *Asteraceae*

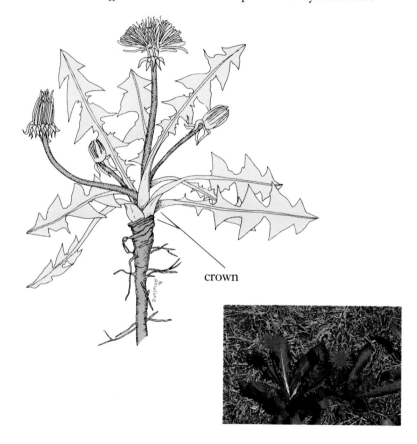

crown

The meaning of the Latin name for this very familiar plant attests to its nutritional value. *Taraxacum offinale* means "official remedy for disorders" referring to the effects of its high vitamin A, calcium and iron content. Historically, it was used as a spring tonic for people who had spent a long winter without any fresh vegetables.

Recipes:
pp. 17, 28,
42

Several species of dandelion exist in the U.S. and all are edible. For the those few unfamiliar with the plant, the dandelion is known by its bright yellow disc-shaped flower head and deep tap root. Dandelion means "teeth of the lion" in French, which refers to its third distinguishing characteristic, its sharply toothed leaves.

The yellow flower heads, harvested in the spring and early summer, make a superb batter-fried fritter (p. 17). Many wild edible guides will tell you that the young leaves, when gathered before the flowers bloom, may be cooked as a green. We find them laden with tannins and therefore too bitter to recommend. Use the roots to make a good coffee-like beverage (p. 28) and serve the root crowns with a Mexican salsa (p.42).

References to dandelions first appeared in 10th century medical journals of Arabian physicians. By the nineteenth century, the plant had become a cooking herb in Europe. Dandelion root has been used by European herbalists for centuries to treat diabetes and liver diseases, and as a diuretic, laxative and appetite stimulant.

Our own colonists first cultivated dandelions in their gardens to use as a potherb, and to supply a constant source of flowers for their beehives. They soon became one of the first of many "garden escaped" plants. The wind ensured that the alien dandelion spread westward rapidly and so helped to sustain the European pioneers on their journey west. Before white settlement, the Apache people of the Southwest used the dandelion as a vegetable.

Dandelions are an alien species to America; they did not originate in this country and are now considered weeds. They were brought to America by European settlers to provide a longer-lasting source of flowers for their bee colonies, for which dandelions are still valuable today. They are so prevalent and bloom so long that they help sustain honeybees between the bloomings of the more coveted but less prolific flowers such as those of apple trees.

Unfortunately, this edible and medicinal plant is almost singularly responsible for the annual use of millions of gallons of lawn herbicides in the U.S. The use of these toxins for want of a perfectly green lawn is seriously detrimental to the environment. If we could change our attitudes about dandelions, we could greatly reduce the use of the herbicides which so negatively impact our Earth.

LAMB'S QUARTERS

Chenopodium album   The Goosefoot family: *Chenopodiaceae*

Dunsmore '91

note
distinctively-
shaped leaves
and powdery
stem

*Recipes:
pp. 29, 43,
44, 61*

If you have a garden, you have likely pulled this edible and added it to the weed pile. You'll want to rethink this practice because lamb's quarters is full of nutrition; in fact, you may have spent hours on your knees weeding out a plant that compares favorably to almost any cultivated vegetable in its vitamin A and vitamin C content. A member of the family of plants which includes beets, swiss chard and spinach, 100 grams (3 1/2 oz) of raw Lamb's quarters contain 11,600 IU (international units) of vitamin A, 1.2 mg of iron, 80 mg of vitamin C; it has no sodium and only 43 calories. Those accustomed to harvesting it call it "wild spinach" and, as with cultivated spinach, the leaves cook down a great deal…be sure to pick plenty of it.

Lamb's quarters is commonly called "goosefoot" or "pigweed" because of the diamond shape of its powdery white leaves. It can grow up to 3 feet tall and is available from early summer until frost throughout the continental U.S. It does flower, but the flowers are green, tiny, and hardly noticeable. What you *will* notice are the large seed clusters which develop from the flowers. The four delicious lamb's quarters recipes in this book use the leaves of the plant, but the seeds are also edible when ground into a nutritious, black flour and mixed with wheat flour. These seeds are an important food source for wildlife; grouse and pheasant feast on this roadside plant in the fall.

Introduced from Europe, lamb's quarters' wind-pollinated seeds spread quickly across the west and provided an important food source for Native Americans. We think Lamb's quarters is one of the most likely Plantworks plants to be cultivated for human consumption in the future.

OAK

Quercus spp.   The Beech Family: *Fagaceae*

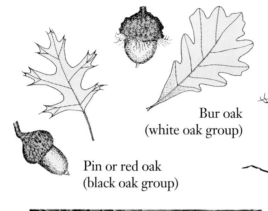

Bur oak
(white oak group)

Pin or red oak
(black oak group)

White oak
silhouette

Recipes:
pp. 14, 15,
24, 25
(see also p.23,
acorn flour)

As a preschooler, you were probably taught that squirrels eat acorns and store them for winter. You probably *didn't* learn that processed acorns can be eaten by people too. Yet, acorns have been eaten by many peoples around the world.

There are over 50 species of oaks in the United States; most of these are found in the East. There are two main groups of oaks, white and black. Red oaks are included in the black group. The white oaks have round, lobed leaves, and generally have light-colored bark. Its acorns mature in one year. The black oaks have pointed lobes, dark colored bark and acorns that mature in two years. All oaks flower in the spring, are wind-pollinated and have edible acorns if properly processed.

Look for acorns in late summer and fall. If your area has experienced a spring drought, the stress caused by a lack of water will reduce the number of white oak acorns that fall. The red oaks should produce the year of the drought, but production will be affected the following year. This balancing act of nature helps to provide continual food resources for wildlife.

Preparing acorns for use in recipes is tedious but harvesting can be done in season and the acorns stored until there is time for shelling and processing. It is important to store the acorns in paper bags and put them in your freezer. They will mold if left in a sealed container at room temperature. See page 23 for information on how to make acorn flour.

Acorns were a major food crop for Native Americans. In season, some tribes gathered four to five hundred pounds a day. Large quantites were needed since one to two pounds of acorns could be consumed by one person in just one day. In 1620, during the Pilgrims' first winter in Massachusetts, the local tribes gave them baskets of acorns which helped to sustain them through the winter. There are records establishing their use as a food source as far back as 2,000 years ago.

Acorns are also one of the most important food crops for wildlife. They are important to deer, squirrels, grouse, pheasants, chipmunks and bear. Keep this in mind so that you do not over-harvest acorns in any one area.

Oaks represent over half of the hardwood timber produced in the U.S. Oak wood is very dense and makes excellent, long-lasting furniture. Most people don't realize that cork is harvested from the bark of oak trees in Europe and Northern Africa. Oaks are also very popular shade trees.

PLANTAIN, COMMON

Plantago major   The Plantain Family: *Plantaginaceae*

flower spike

gather younger
leaves

*Recipes:
pp. 30, 45,
62*

Found throughout North America in several species, this is a plant of many names and an interesting history. It was unknown in North America until European settlers arrived. The seeds of this low basal-leaved plant came over in the hooves of oxen and horses, so you can guess why one of its nicknames became "white-man's footstep." It's also called "Lyre's weed" because of its resemblance to the stringed instrument of the same name. In more recent tradition, young people finding it along paths in the woods pull apart the plantain leaf and see who gets the longest "string" and so is the biggest "liar."

You can locate plantain by looking for its oval or spade-shaped basal leaves which grow low to the ground. Start looking for this good source of vitamins A and C in late spring, before it grows to its full height of 6-18". When you harvest the nut-flavored leaves for trail nibbles and salads, it is important that you pick the leaves *young* and *small*. If you want to harvest the older leaves, cook them to avoid the bitter taste that comes with age. If you are using Plantworks with young people and they're not particularly fond of green vegetables, we suggest the appealing cheese pie, recipe p. 30.

The Saxons considered plantain one of the nine sacred herbs; they referred to plantain as the "mother of herbs" as its crushed leaves were used for cuts, sores, burns and snake bites. Roots were chewed to relieve toothaches. A tea made from its seeds was used for diarrhea and ulcers, and the cooled teas served as an astringent. In 1687 a report from Virginia stated that the local Native Americans referred to it as "Englishman's Foot" and made a diuretic tea from its leaves and a dull gold dye from the entire plant.

PURSLANE

Portulaca oleracea   The Purslane family: *Portulacaceae*

note
reddish
stem

thick, fleshy
leaves

Recipes:
pp. 18, 31,
63, 64, 65

Like lamb's quarters, this overlooked 'sidewalk species' is very nutritious but is usually pulled from gardens as a nuisance, even though for 2,000 years it has been a food crop in its native India and Persia (now Iran). Introduced to Europe and the Americas, it has not caught on in the U.S. as an edible plant in spite of its high nutritive value and its presence in all 50 states. Purslane is still sold in Mexican markets today.

To encourage you to collect this garden gem, we offer you this: a 100 gram (3 1/2 oz) portion of purslane contains 21 calories, 1.4 g of protein, .4 g of fat, 2,500 I.U. (international units) of vitamin A, 25 mg of vitamin C and 3.5 mg of iron. It has been recommended by the U.S. Department of Agriculture for cultivation as a potherb.

You can select this plant when you don't have time to travel to a wooded or marshy area since it will literally be in your own back yard. It grows in roadside/waste areas and around sidewalks in sandy soils. Look for a small sprawling plant with light green rounded leaves, a reddish stem and five-petaled small yellow flowers that open only on bright sunny days. To be sure that you have properly identified purslane, note that its stem is *not* hairy and that the leaves are fleshy, not thin and papery. Be sure to wash it well, as sand tends to stick to the plant. The leaves do not cook down and therefore you do not need to collect more than you'll need for your recipe. The leaves are good additions to soups and stews.

Like most of these prolific Plantworks plants, purslane came to America during colonial times. It has been documented that in the early 1600's Native Americans in Maine were growing purslane along with corn. It spread so quickly across the Americas that by the mid-1600's purslane was being cultivated in Brazil.

Purslane is also of value to wildlife. Animals ranging from small rodents to song birds depend on the plentiful seeds and succulent leaves. These seeds can be collected and ground into a rich black flour. A diligent researcher counted 52,300 seeds on one plant!

RED CLOVER

Trifolium pratense   The Bean Family: *Fabaceae*

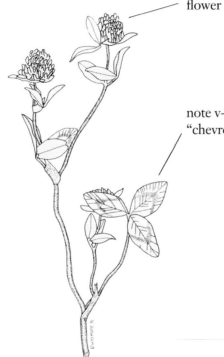

flower head

note v-shaped "chevron" on leaves

Recipes: pp. 19, 46, 47

If you are new to harvesting wild edibles and you don't have a naturalist to guide you, you may feel confident beginning with red clover. The red clover plant is common in fields and wayside areas and you can probably find it in your lawn. You may already be familiar with its reddish compact flower head and groups of three leaves, each with white v-shaped 'chevrons'. Only the flower head is edible.

Use the flower heads for fritters just like you would the dandelion, or use it for making teas and jellies. Red clover tea is excellent for warming friends on a winter day. Harvest the flowers in full bloom and dry on a screen in a cool dry place or in a food dehydrator (see p. 142). An easy drying method is simply putting the harvested clover heads into a brown paper bag and leaving them in the refrigerator for three days. Store in a dry place for winter use. They will keep this way for years and you need only to invest in a tea-ball to enjoy this hot beverage on a cold winter evening. If you don't want to wait until winter to try it, ice it and add a mint leaf for a refreshing summer drink. It only takes three or four flowers to make one cup of tea. Medicinally, red clover tea has been used to help coughs, colds and sore throats.

Many old songs and stories refer to the luck which a four-leaved clover will bring you. It is hard to determine exactly where and when this superstition started, but all clovers were once thought to give protection against witchcraft and evil spirits. When travelers crossed areas thought to house evil spirits, they often carried several stalks of red clover in their pockets for protection. A four-leaved clover results from a mutation. These plants commonly have leaves in groupings of three—the translation of its botanical name is "three-leaves of the meadows."

If you've read about other Plantworks plants, you'll notice that many of these very common wild edible plants are not native. Brought over from Europe and Asia for hay and forage for which it is still commonly used by farmers, red clover now grows wild throughout the continental U.S. It has over 75 subspecies, and is the state flower of Vermont.

STINGING NETTLES

Urtica dioica   The Nettle Family : *Urticaceae*

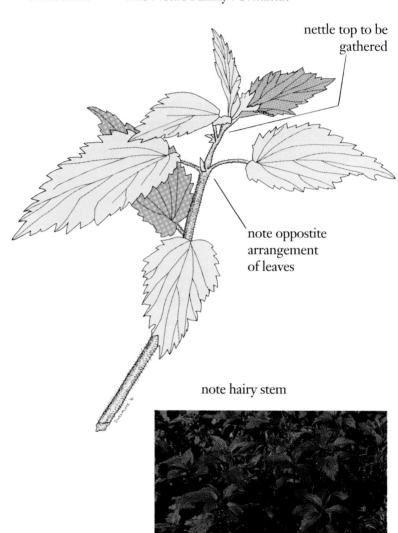

nettle top to be
gathered

note oppostite
arrangement
of leaves

note hairy stem

Recipes:
pp. 48, 49,
50

If you are unaware of the nutritious and terrific-tasting recipes which can be made from this plant, you probably regard it as the reason first-aid ointment was invented. Yes, stinging nettles are covered with minute stinging hairs containing formic acid, which cause an instant rash when brushed against exposed skin. Its Latin name "*dioica*" actually means "big sting." Don't be alarmed. Cooking this plant eliminates the water-soluble acid.

Find this common, inconspicuous plant in moist, disturbed transition areas throughout the eastern United States. Stinging nettle is an erect, 2-4' tall plant. Its toothed leaves are arranged opposite each other along a grooved stem. Clusters of tiny, nondescript, light green drooping flowers occur at each leaf axil. The flowers, although not colorful or showy, do attract insects. Wind pollination is the primary method by which the plant is propagated. Harvest this gourmet-quality edible in the spring and summer. Donned in gloves, choose only the easily removable tops for the Plantworks recipes.

You'll enjoy serving nettles to your family as a cooked vegetable or soup. Euell Gibbons noted its high nutritional value in a 1966 analysis; it has vitamins A and C and iron and more protein than any other known leafy vegetable, 6.9% per 100 grams of the fresh greens.

A popular medicinal herb and food in the British Isles, it has yet to acquire popularity in the U.S. Traditionally, a nettle tea has been considered a cure for just about everything from gout and rheumatism to nosebleeds and dandruff. A green dye may be extracted from this versatile plant. Historically, the use of nettles as a fiber source can be traced to the Bronze age; "nettles" means "textile plant." Nettles were cultivated in Scotland for their stem fibers, which were made into a durable linen-like cloth.

A similar plant, wood nettle (*Laportea candensis*) is also found throughout woodlands of the eastern United States. This nettle is different in that its leaves are alternately attached, but both nettles have similar uses.

SUMAC

Rhus spp. The Cashew Family: *Anacardiaceae*

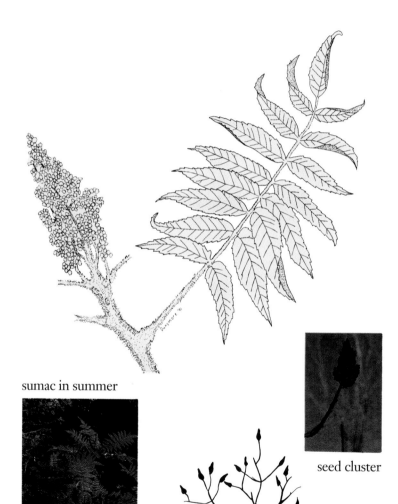

sumac in summer

seed cluster

winter silhouette
of entire plant

Recipes:
pp. 20, 51,
66

When we mention sumac as food, people frequently say, "Isn't that a poisonous plant?" There *is* a species of sumac called poison sumac (*Rhus Vernix*), but it is easily distinguishable from both the smooth sumac (*Rhus glabra*) and the staghorn sumac (*Rhus typhina*). Smooth and staghorn sumac seeds are red and non-poisonous; the plants are found in well-drained soils. On the other hand, poison sumac seeds are white and the plants are found in moist shady areas. Because of these obvious differences, you'll be able to easily distinguish between the two.

We use smooth and staghorn sumac, both found throughout the eastern United States. Both staghorn and smooth sumac grow in old fields and dry transition areas and are considered invader plants, or ones which begin the process of succession of an open grassy area into a woodland. The two common names refer to the woody shrubs' smooth or fuzzy branches, which grow up to 20 feet high. Note the compound (multiple) leaves and tiny red fuzzy seeds; they form tight clusters in the staghorn and loose clusters in the smooth. Sumac shrubs have female and male flowers on separate plants. Female flowers become the red clusters of seeds.

The processed seeds are the only parts of this plant which are edible. Harvest sumac seeds when they are red and tart. The hairs on each seed are covered with malic acid which lends them their tartness. Sample one seed of a cluster to determine tartness; bland-tasting seeds will produce poor-quality drinks and jellies. The seeds must be rinsed and strained through a cheese cloth before eating. Sumac jelly (p. 51) is a favorite of those with a sweet tooth and the sumac summer refresher (p. 66) is a fun alternative to soda. Sumac seeds remain over winter and are one of the few plant products which can be harvested at that time of year. The furry sumac fruits are favorites among the birds and squirrels.

Many people know sumac as one of the first plants to turn color in the fall. Its orange-red leaves are a brilliant signal that autumn is on its way. Some Native American tribes used the sumac stems in making ceremonial pipes. Stems were split, hollowed, and rejoined to create the stem of the pipe. They dried the sumac leaves for use as tobacco, a practice that continues today among some tribes.

WILD GRAPE

Vitus spp.   The Grape Family: *Vitaceae*

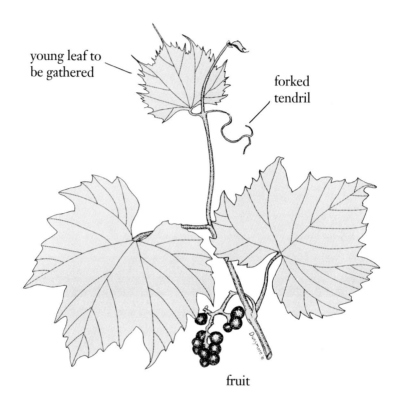

young leaf to
be gathered

forked
tendril

fruit

young leaves and
tendrils

Recipes:
pp. 32, 52,
67

Wild grape is an exceptional plant to get to know because its leaves, tendrils and berries are all edible. Because it has several edible plant parts which are available during different seasons, the wild grape is the "cattail" of woodland edges. Wild grape is abundant throughout the United States and all of its many species are edible. Make sure the plant you've found has all of these three major characteristics: forked tendrils, stalked leaves and toothed leaf edges. If the plant is missing any of these characteristics, it might be a poisonous plant called "moonseed." Moonseed fruit contains several *crescent-shaped* seeds whereas wild grapes hold many *pear-shaped* seeds. These two plants are easily distinguishable, and it is important to make note of these features, especially when harvesting with young people.

Virginia creeper (*Parthenocissus quinquefolia*) is a vine that often grows in the same vicinity as wild grape. It is similar to wild grape in that it does have a dark purplish fruit, but the similarity ends there. Virginia creeper has a five-part palmately compound leaf (separate leaflets attached at a central stem) and has no forked tendrils. Its fruits are sparse clusters with distinctively red stems. The most important thing to keep in mind when picking a vine is to make sure that you untangle the vines so that you don't pick the wrong plant.

The berries of the wild grape are ready to harvest when dark-bluish purple, but they are really too tart to use as a trail nibble. The young tendrils can be chewed for their tangy flavor. The leaves are delicious when used in our recipes (pp. 32 and 67) and young people will enjoy making and eating wild grape jelly (p. 52).

The wild grape is a very famous fruiting plant with a long history. Like all domesticated fruits and vegetables, table grapes and wine grapes were once wild. Grapes were cultivated in the Old World over 7,000 years ago. Grape leaves have long been used by the Greeks in entrees where the leaves are stuffed with lamb or beef. European grape species were unsuccessful when first introduced to cultivation in the United States although many Old-World varieties have since been successfully grown in California and elsewhere. Popular native varieties such as Concord, Isabella and Catawba were derived from wild American species.

WILD ROSE

Rosa spp.   The Rose Family: *Rosaceae*

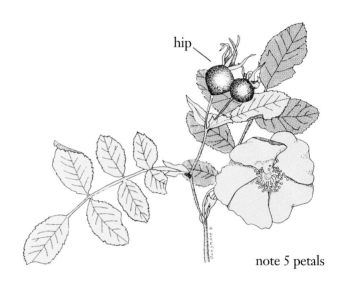

hip

note 5 petals

Recipes:
pp. 53, 54,
68

Our modern floral rose was cultivated from wild roses which grow abundantly in openlands and roadsides. The 3,000 species of wild rose worldwide all share the basic rose characteristics of five petals, five sepals and alternate leaves. The three most common species are the wrinkled rose, the pasture rose and the sweetbrier rose. The familiar wild rose, a thorny relative of the apple tree, is also related to the strawberry, raspberry, cherry, plum, peach, almond, pear and crabapple.

The petals and hips of all of the rose species are edible. In the spring, harvest the flower petals of the wild rose and add them to salads for color. Use the rose hip to convince those hesitant to eat wild foods that it really is a rewarding experience.

The hip, also called the "haw," is the part of the flower which forms fruit after the flower is pollinated and the petals have dropped. It looks like a swelling at the base of the flower, and is about 1/4" to 1" in diameter. When rose hips turn from green to red, they are edible. To eat the hip raw, split it open with your fingernail, remove and discard the seeds, and eat. In harvesting, be careful of the prickles which occur in varying densities on the stems of roses. These annoying projections are really superficial stem tissue growth which arm the plant and reduce browsing by wildlife. The rose hip is an overwintering fruit which helps to sustain birds, squirrels and even deer in the barren winter season. Apply the rule of 10 by harvesting only one rose hip for every ten you leave behind.

Save the jelly-making recipes for days when you have more time and have the proper jars and ingredients. The steps in the jelly making process lend themselves well to working with small groups.

Rose hips contain 60 times as much vitamin C as oranges, gram for gram. In Europe, during the shortages of World War II, it protected people from scurvy (a disease caused by lack of vitamin C). Europeans today use a purée of rose hips called "Nyppon Sopa" as a cold remedy. Rose hip tea is commonly found in grocery stores.

The wild rose is the state flower of Iowa and North Dakota. A major perfume industry started around the wild rose in Bulgaria and surrounding countries. The extracted Damask Rose oil "Attar" is still in use in the perfume industry today.

WINTER CRESS

Barbarea vulgaris The Mustard Family: *Brassicaceae*

yellow
flowers

note distinctive
shape of basal leaves
and terminal lobe

Winter cress, while being a plant in the mustard family (*Brassicaceae*), is not a true mustard. True mustards (*Brassica*) share the genus with plants such as brussels sprouts, broccoli and turnips. Winter cress (*Barbarea*) has features similar to these plants, but its unique seed pod shape places it in this separate genus. All members of the mustard family, including winter cress, can be identified by four petals in the shape of a cross and six stamens, four long and two short. Winter cress grows to the height of two feet.

Look for winter cress in recently disturbed, moist ground areas throughout eastern and central United States. Winter cress is a fairly inconspicuous plant until it flowers in spring. You'll first notice the small clusters of yellow flowers, each cluster measuring one-half inch across. Its basal leaves are characterized by three to six distinct lobes on each side (lateral) of the midrib and one large lobe on the end (terminal lobe); see illustration. Its seed pods, measuring only one inch and pointing upwards, contain small black seeds resembling pepper which can be used as a pepper substitute.

The young leaves are delicious when eaten raw. Older leaves are also good tasting when cooked as a green in several changes of water. Harvest early in the cool spring months since in warm weather the leaves become quite bitter tasting. This wild edible is a good choice for those eager to get outdoors right away in the early spring. Once you properly identify this plant, you'll notice how common it is along roadsides.

So why call a plant winter cress when it blooms in the spring? In Europe, where the plant originates, and where winter temperatures are relatively warm, winter cress is known to bloom even in December. December 4th was celebrated as St. Barbarea's Day and winter cress was the only edible plant available for harvesting at the time. Hence both its Latin and common names.

A similar edible species, early winter cress (*Barbarea verna*), is found from New York to Florida. Called scurvy grass in the south, it differs only in its additional leaf lobes. It is still sold in some East-coast markets as a potherb and salad ingredient.

YELLOW WOOD SORREL

Oxalis stricta   The Wood-sorrel Family : *Oxalidaceae*

fruit

yellow
flower

note clover-shaped leaves

You'll recognize this common backyard and roadside plant by its tiny, clover-like leaves and its equally tiny five-petaled yellow flowers. Native to both North America and Europe, yellow wood sorrel is often found growing in sidewalk cracks. It's a conveniently available wild edible when you don't want to leave the neighborhood but want to have a non-traditional treat.

Yellow wood sorrel grows throughout the eastern United States and extends to Arizona and Colorado. It is a highly variable species, but it always grows in clusters and its fruit always extends upward and outward. When it goes to seed, the beak-like projections look and taste like sour pickles. Wood sorrel leaves have a sour flavor and should be harvested when the leaves are young and light green. Yellow Wood Sorrel is quite versatile as it can be used in soups, stews, salads, and as an iced tea.

Yellow wood sorrel was a popular herb sauce and salad ingredient in Elizabethan times. The genus name *Oxalis* is derived from the Greek word for sharp, referring to the sour taste of its leaves. It also refers to the oxalic acid which is contained in its leaves; eating excessive amounts of the raw leaves may cause stomach upset due to this acid. Wood sorrel was effective in treating inflammatory problems, fevers, kidney and bladder troubles because of its high content of vitamin C, phosphorus and potassium.

Much of what we are learning as "new" edible plants is actually rediscovery. Since many of the plants introduced in Plantworks were once well-respected and eagerly sought as food, it seems our challenge is to change our attitudes about what we consider "weeds" and what we consider food.

PLANTWORKS
ACTIVITIES

Hiking helpers *(pp.106-109)*
Helpful hints for hiking with a group

While You Wait *(pp. 110-120)*
Fun games and puzzles to do while your creation is in the oven.

Extended Activities *(pp. 121-146)*
Extended craft activities for reinforcing the recognition of the Plantworks plants.

This section is written especially for those of you who are supervising children. With planning, these activity pages can reinforce what the children have learned about the plant world and promote plant recognition. For example, you and your group may want to learn about cattails from the natural history section, hike to harvest some, cook cattail corn-on-the-cob and then make cattail placemats.

Each recipe is cross-referenced with the activity and natural history sections to make the selection of activites easier. Included with each "Extended Activity" are the estimated completion time, cost and recommended age level. When completed, some crafts like the mini plant press can be useful in future hikes.

We have taken an ecological approach to the craft activities by suggesting the use of non-toxic products and reusable materials whenever possible. These activity pages are intended for your convenient use. You may copy them as needed for the use of your family, class, or group, without permission from the publisher.

HIKING HELPERS

Most often your hike to harvest wild edibles will consist of a trip to your garden or backyard. When it involves a fairly lengthy excursion you may want to make it more exciting and educational by doing some of the following activities along the way.

The simplest way for leaders to enhance a wild foods expedition is to bring *Plantworks* along and read parts of the natural history information to your group in some beautiful area prior to locating the plant. After showing them the illustration and photograph and reading about its habitat, they should be able to lead you right to the plant.

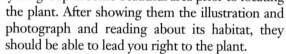

Be sure to check with the local government that the areas where you have decided to harvest have not been sprayed with herbicides. Your inquiries just may help curb the use of these environmentally detrimental sprays!

Here is a list of activities that take little or no preparation and can be done while hiking:

- ***Leaf and Bark Rubbings***

Bring paper and crayons without wrappers to make leaf and bark rubbing. You'll see the uniqueness of different barks. Note the differences between basswood, oak and the other deciduous trees.

- ***Counting Hike***

Predict and then count and keep track of:

- different nature sounds
- different colors in nature
- the most common wild animals (don't forget insects)
- the number of animal homes (holes in trees, nests, holes in the ground)

- ***Predict the Pollinator***

As you hike, discuss the role played by insects, birds and the wind in pollinating flowers. Have your group note the variety of bees, flies, butterflies, beetles, hummingbirds and moths visiting the flowers.

Soon you'll notice that the hummingbirds can be found on the tubular flowers, butterflies will be on those which allow it to grab on with its feet and the others are found on the white and brightly colored flowers. The dull green flowers of plants like plantain and nettles will not have pollinating insects; they are small and pollinated by the wind.

Each time you hike look for flowers, predict their pollinator and then confirm your predictions by observation. Even if your group makes a few wrong guesses, they'll enjoy seeing the insects or birds sampling nectar and spreading pollen.

• Bird Song Hike

Many birds eat berries and pass the seeds through their bodies as they fly. They are important seed dispersers of wild plants and it's fun to learn their calls.

Like fingerprints, each species of songbird has its own unique call. Bird calls are especially prevalent in the spring when birds are staking out their territories and calling for a mate. Follow the less timid birds and take turns trying to imitate them. You'll not only learn their call, but you may see them approach you thinking you are a bird! To remember their calls, think of them as patterns of English words. The phoebe and some of the other songbirds got their names from their calls. The phoebe's call sounds like the words "Fee-bee."

• Poetry Hike

There's a side to hikes that's hard to plan activities for: the silent lack of activity inspired by a deep woods, a quiet stream, or an open meadow. Guiding children through the writing of poetry is one way to help them appreciate this side of the outdoors. Prepare the members of your group for a poetry exercise by asking them to sit or stand and listen and watch for about 5 minutes once you get to a natural area. Ask them to offer suggestions to fill in the blanks of a skeleton poem you prepare; for example,

> Habitat name
> Three words to describe it
> Two phrases that describe how you feel about it
> I wish...

They may end up something like this:

> PRAIRIE
> DRY, GRASSY, BUGGY
> MAKES ME THINK OF BUFFALO DAYS
> AND ENDLESS HORIZONS
> I WISH THEY WOULDN'T DISAPPEAR

Read the resulting poem aloud to your group. They might like it enough to include it in the recycled paper photo cards they make on page 122.

• *Plantworks Bingo*

Play this bingo game while you hike. Instead of a caller calling out letters, have the children use a pencil or crayon to mark off the plants as they spot them. To encourage even more cooperation and less waste of paper, give every two kids one copy of the bingo sheet. On long hikes have them keep track of how many of each plant they see. Pre-schoolers to third graders enjoy this activity.

B	I	N	G	O
CURLY DOCK	RED CLOVER	SUMAC	OPENLAND	BIRD (SEED DISPERSER)
WILD GRAPE	ACORN	PLANTAIN	WILD ROSE	RED OAK TREE
BUTTERFLY (POLLINATOR)	FREE	COMMON DANDELION	WHITE OAK TREE	STINGING NETTLES
YELLOW WOOD SORREL	CATTAIL	WETLAND	FREE	BASS-WOOD
PURSLANE	TRANSITION	LAMB'S QUARTERS	WINTER CRESS	WOODLAND

P

L

A

N

T

WHILE YOU WAIT

Activities to do when the cooking is in progress

While your group anxiously waits for their food to bake or boil, keep them occupied with these activities. You'll maintain control, keep their interest and avoid potential chaos. Even if you do not have a waiting period for your particular recipe, the kids will finish their jobs in the kitchen at different times. The word scrambles and word finds can be handed out to each child as they finish.

COLOR AND IDENTIFY

Answers on p. 119

FLOWER BUILDER

(just like hangman)

Select the name of a Plantworks plant, count the number of letters in the name and draw that number of blanks on the board or on a large piece of paper. As the children take turns guessing a letter to fill the blanks, add a new part to a flower for any incorrectly guessed letters. This is played just like "hangman" and if the whole flower is drawn before the group guesses the plant, you tricked them!

Make the flower you draw resemble a wood sorrel like the one on this page. After playing this game your group will always be able to recognize this plant! Allow eight guesses by drawing the flower in the following order:

1) flower center

2) five petals (one petal per incorrect guess)

3) stem

4) leaf

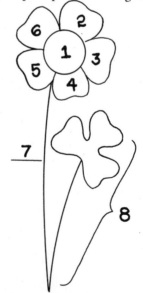

Leaves are attached to plants in specific, definite ways. Go through *Plantworks'* illustrations for all fifteen plants and determine which type of leaf attachment each one has. Then match each one to the right example.

Basswood

Cattail

Curled Dock

Dandelion

Lamb's Quarters

Oak

Plantain

Purslane

Red Clover

Stinging Nettles

Sumac

Wild Grape

Wild Rose

Winter Cress

Yellow Wood Sorrel

Aternate
Leaf Arrangement

Opposite
Leaf Arrangement

Basal
Leaf Arrangement

WORD FINDS

Answers on p. 119

```
D C H A M A M S A P D A W H E E L I N S
L O D D I M E A K U L A M B L I O N S D
S M O U T I L K O R A S N U S S E E N B
X M A W I L D R O S E S S E L K R T D F
V O R T S M A N D L R E T N I C O T H E
E N H C I S Q C G A T H E N R O L L P D
P D A L M A A S S N A B F E A M H E L R
A A Y I L M P B O E E G T C B W X S A Y
R N P I U V A I N O O N L I N P N E N D
G D Y S W T I H E S I L E A R S T N T H
D E E R E M S I P W L H E R E E W I A F
L L L A N D U D C S R E A N D E D L I W
I I N F N O G U A G A R R A C W O O N S
W O O D C A R O T V E R A R L D E G F U
S N W I Z L K J T D D E T R O U Q D F E
A S S N Y O I T A A I L R A V S K N U P
S C U D F E C E I I R E I L E B D R G O
R G O A K I A N L K R E M W R L I O N O
S C A R E D Y C A T A G E N T C O C O P
K A L A M B S Q U A R T E R S D E A F W
```

Acorn	Plantain
Basswood	Purslane
Cattail	Red Clover
Common Dandelion	Sumac
Curly Dock	Wild Grape
Lambs Quarters	Wild Rose
Nettles	Winter Cress
Oak	Wood Sorrel

```
A X O X A L I S S T R I C T A T E N A T
C R F S D Q V R I R O R I P S Y C H B A
T C B H E K O O V T E C U P A P R I A R
R M H A S E H S A R R I S L O H E A R A
I R T I L I A A M E R I C A N A L A B X
F I Z I N G B W O O D L A N H L O X A A
O C H D A R S B L E S R E T S A S Z R C
L N N I E M C U O K I N T A O T K R E U
I G U E R N A V H W E R V G O I K I A M
U A U C A F R A N R U C E O G F O C V O
M E R R M A V N Y M U R D E L O A P U F
P L A N T A G E E N E T D E R L E R L F
R C U B B I T X E M A R I M P I R O G I
A S Y M P T C O T V I T U S L A A V A C
T E R R A R P A I N S W E A U T Z S R I
E M E A I I S L E S D E D U M C K R I N
N D U S P L U R I B U S S U C A R H S A
S L P O R T U L A C A O L E R A C E A L
E U P A R S T U L C I O N E B A K A U E
S T C H E N O P O D I U M A L B U M S Q
```

Barbarea Vulgaris
Chenopodium Album
Oxalis Stricta
Plantago
Portulaca Oleracea
Quercus
Rhus Glabra
Rosa

Rumex Crispus
Taraxacum Officinale
Tilia Americana
Trifolium Pratense
Typha Latifolia
Urtica
Vitus

CROSSWORD PUZZLE

Answers on p. 120

Use the Natural History section to help you with this.

Across

1. Ground-up acorns, for instance

3. What you probably used to think many Plantworks plants were

5. ___land: habitat like fields, gardens, and empty lots

8. Its beak-shaped seeds taste like sour pickles

11. The color of ripe sumac seeds

12. Squirrels love it

14. Produces 12 Across

15. How you hear birdsongs

16. The only "mustard" in *Plantworks*

18. The direction you turn your stove's switch to cook

20. "Step lightly on the ____"

21. ____land: marshy habitat

22. Leaf divisions (oak leaf "points" for instance)

24. Also called "goosefoot"

26. Its Latin name is *Rumex Crispus*

29. Many use harmful chemicals to get rid of these

Down

2. Look for chevrons on this lucky plants leaves

3. The only vine in *Plantworks*

4. New young growth on a plant

6. This sidewalk species grows in all 50 states

7. Native Americans called this "white man's foot"

Down, continued

8. The only plant with thorns in *Plantworks*

9. Two varieties are staghorn and smooth

10. Wear gloves to harvest this one

13. Habitat found where fields become woods

16. Habitat with many trees

17. *Plantworks'* only wetland plant

19. The "leaf" of a flower

23. You may need a ladder to reach these flowers

25. What you eat soup with

27. The underground part of a plant

28. When put in the ground, it may become a plant

SCRAMBLED WORDS

Answers on p. 119

118

1. SOADWBDS

  _ _ _ _ _ _ _ _

2. CUAMS

  _ _ _ _ _

3. DLWI ESRO

  _ _ _ _   _ _ _ _

4. DOWO LEROSR

  _ _ _ _ _   _ _ _ _ _ _

5. KAO NCRAO

  _ _ _   _ _ _ _ _

6. LICTAAT

  _ _ _ _ _ _ _

7. RTIWEN SRESC

  _ _ _ _ _ _ _   _ _ _ _ _

8. NOMCMO NONEDDAIL

  _ _ _ _ _ _   _ _ _ _ _ _ _ _ _ _

9. BLASM SQRARTUE

  _ _ _ _ _   _ _ _ _ _ _ _ _

10. TNETSLE

  _ _ _ _ _ _ _

11. NIAPALNT

  _ _ _ _ _ _ _ _

12. ESRPALUN

  _ _ _ _ _ _ _ _

13. DRE VREOLC

  _ _ _   _ _ _ _ _ _

14. DWLI EPAGR

  _ _ _ _   _ _ _ _ _

15. DCERUL KODC

  _ _ _ _ _ _   _ _ _ _

ANSWERS

Word Finds, pp. 114-115

```
D  C                     P                          S
   O                     U                      N  S
   M  O                  R                      E
   M     W  I  L  D  R  O  S  E              R  T
   O        S           L                 C     T
E  N           S  C     A              R     L  P
P  D              A     N        E           E  L
A  A        M     B     E     T              S  A
R  N     U              N                       N
G  D  S                    I              R     T
D  E                 W  L                 E     A
L  L              C        E           D        I
I  I              U  A        R        C        N
W  O        R     T        R     R  L
   N        L     T                    O
        Y        A                 V  S     N
     D           I                 E     D  R
     O  A  K     L                 R        O
   C                                     C  O
K  L  A  M  B  S  Q  U  A  R  T  E  R  S     A     W
```

```
A     O  X  A  L  I  S  S  T  R  I  C  T  A  T           T
   R                 R                    Y        B     A
T     B              O              P  P        A     R
R        A           S              L  H        R     A
I     T  I  L  I  A  A  M  E  R  I  C  A  N  A     B     X
F           G                       N     L     A     A
O              S                    T     A     R     C
L                 U                 A     T     E     U
I                    H     R  G     I     I     A     M
U     U                 R  U        O     F     V     O
M        R              M           O     O     U     F
P        T        I     E           L     L     L     F
R           I     X                 I           G     I
A           C     V  I  T  U  S     A           A     C
T           R  A              U                 R     I
E           I                       C           I     N
N        S                                R     S     A
S     P  O  R  T  U  L  A  C  A  O  L  E  R  A  C  E  A  L
E  U                                            U     E
S     C  H  E  N  O  P  O  D  I  U  M  A  L  B  U  M     Q
```

Scrambled Words, p. 118

1. Basswood
2. Sumac
3. Wild Rose
4. Wood Sorrel
5. Oak Acorn
6. Cattail
7. Winter Cress
8. Common Dandelion
9. Lamb's Quarters
10. Nettles
11. Plantain
12. Purslane
13. Red Clover
14. Wild Grape
15. Curled Dock

Color and Identify, p. 111

1. White Oak
2. Sumac
3. Basswood
4. Curled Dock

Crossword, pp 116-117

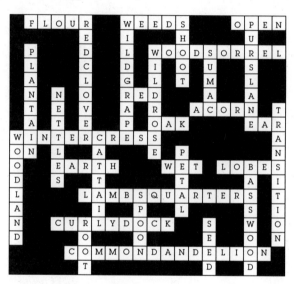

Leaf Attachment, p. 113

Basswood: Alternate
Cattail: Basal
Curled Dock: Alternate & Basal
Dandelion: Basal
Lamb's Quarters: Alternate
Oak: Alternate
Plantain: Basal
Purslane: Alternate

Red Clover: Alternate
Stinging Nettles: Opposite
Sumac: Alternate
Wild Grape: Alternate & Opposite
Wild Rose: Alternate
Winter Cress: Alternate & Basal
Yellow Wood Sorrel: Alternate

EXTENDED ACTIVITIES

Activities to do when the cooking is through

The following activities are designed to encourage and reinforce the identification of the fifteen Plantworks wild edibles in a fun hands-on way. After you have done some cooking with your group, choose from these related craft ideas. Note that the completion time, cost and recommended age have been listed for every activity.

We have made an effort to offer activities which minimize the harvesting of great quantities of plants and which encourage the reuse of items rather than the purchase of new craft materials.

Cost
UNDER
$2

Time
20
MINS.

Ages
8 & up

LEAF-RUBBING PHOTO CARD

What you'll need (per person):

1 sheet	8 1/2 x 11" recycled bond paper
1	3 1/2 x 5" photograph (use a favorite)
1 leaf	from a Plantworks plant
1	crayon with paper wrapping removed
1	scissors/craft knife
1	large paper clip
1	permanent marking pen
1	pencil

Here's how:

Fold sheet of paper in half so the ends meet, and then fold the halved sheet in half once more. Turn it so it opens like a greeting card.

Place leaf, vein side up, under one layer of paper (the front cover of the card). Hold it in place with paper clip. Rub over leaf with side of crayon until entire leaf shows through. Label leaf with both its common and its Latin name using a marking pen. Oak, basswood and grapevine work well in leaf rubbings.

Open card. Place the photo you've selected so that it is centered on the facing page. Using a pencil, lightly trace the corners of the photo onto the card. Cut diagonal slits 1/4" inside each of the corners so that the photo can be slipped into place.

Now write your own message appropriate to the occasion under the photo or on the facing page. The result? A home-made greeting card which is recycled and teaches the receiver about a wild plant!

Cost
UNDER
$2

Time
20
MINS.
+ 2 hrs in
the middle

Ages
9 & up

CHOCOLATE LEAVES

Wild plants for the junk-food junkie

Here's a change. You are about to take a healthy low-calorie wild plant and turn it into junk food. Nevertheless, it *is* a fun hands-on experience that will help you to remember the intricacies of leaves.

We recommend the following leaves for this project: all grape leaves, large lamb's quarter leaves, the basal or bottom winter cress leaves, and any leaves of plantain, oak or basswood. Some leaves do have toxins in them so make sure of your choice; even if you are only using the leaf as a base for the chocolate, the chocolate could absorb the toxins.

What you'll need:

1	unblemished leaf for each person
1-2 oz	chocolate pieces per person*
1	artist's paint brush (never used with paints)
	waxed paper

* 1 lb. of chocolate should be plenty for a group of 12 if each is doing one leaf.

Here's how:

To make a carbon copy of the leaf you wish to remember:

1) Wash and pat dry a good specimen of your leaf.

2) Melt chocolate, preferably in a double boiler. If the chocolate needs thinning, add a few drops of vegetable oil, not water. Watered chocolate will not adhere to leaves and may crack off.

3) Taking a clean small paintbrush, paint the back side of each leaf. The back side will give a better image. Try not to let the chocolate get on the front of the leaf.

4) Put the coated leaf on a small piece of waxed paper and chill in the refrigerator for several hours. The freezer will speed up the process but frozen chocolate has a tendency to crack easily.

5) Beginning at the petiole or leaf stem, gently pull each leaf away from the chocolate.

6) Keep the chocolate leaves in your refrigerator until you are ready to eat them. They can be used to decorate cakes and cupcakes for special occasions.

WILD (ROSE) CUPCAKES

Cost
UNDER
$5

Time
15
MINS.

Ages
4 & up

Here's a quick and easy edible project to do for a special treat for your group. Doing this before harvesting hips for jelly and tea will help your group learn to identify the wild rose plant.

What you'll need for 3-4 cupcakes:

3-4	cupcakes
20	rose petals
1	egg white
1/4 cup	sugar
	mixer
	bowl
	food coloring
	decorative cake
	toppings

Here's how:

1. Wash rose and separate into individual petals and pat dry.

2. Separate egg(s) and beat egg white(s) until stiff and frothy. Add a few drops of food coloring.

3. Carefully dip the petals into the beaten whites and set on plate.

4. Sprinkle sugar and decorative candies over the petals.

5. Arrange back into the shape of a flower and place on frosted cupcakes or cakes (bake your own or buy plain frosted cupcakes).

SAVE-A-TREE
WRAPPING PAPER

Kids love doing this project. It's a quick and easy way to make gifts more personal.

Doing this project in December before the holiday season, is timely and practical. Gift wrap, used one time to conceal gifts, is an expensive waste of natural resources and landfill space.

What you'll need:

1	brayer (artist's roller)
	non-toxic water-soluble paint
1	piece of plate glass (8 1/2 x 11" or larger)
	brown paper bags or newsprint (to be printed)
	scrap newspapers
	leaves from Plantworks plants (wild grape, oak, basswood and leaflet of sumac work best)
1	laundry marking pen
1	scissors
1	clean rag

Here's how:

Have kids wear old clothes or full aprons. Tape newspaper down to the table to protect it. If you are making the wrapping paper out of shopping bags, slit them open so you can print the inside.

1. Place teaspoon of paint on the glass.

2. Roll brayer in the paint until it is fully covered.

3. Place leaf front side down onto the glass. "Ink" the back side of the leaf until no part of the original color of the leaf is showing. It should be covered but not gloppy.

4. Place leaf paint side down on your selected fabric.

5. Cover with clean piece of newspaper and press carefully with your fingers until ink is transferred to fabric.

6. After leaf print is dry to the touch, neatly print the name of the plant under the leaf.

You can use the same method to make *Plantworks* T-shirts for your group. Make sure to use textile ink and put a layer of newspaper inside the shirt before you print it. Also, press the shirts with an iron before washing them to prevent the ink from washing out.

HOLD THOSE RECIPES

with a tile recipe card holder

Kids of all ages will enjoy this one. It's easy to do and makes a practical gift for all cooks who tend to spill or lose their recipes in the middle of cooking!

What you'll need:

1   tile per child (go to a tile shop and ask for their discontinued stock)

2   springed clothes pins per holder
        white glue
        acrylic paints
        paint brush

Cost
UNDER
$2

Time
45
MINS.

Ages
8 & up

Here's how:

Decorate the tile and allow it to dry before assembling the holder. To decorate the tile, use one of the following depending on the age and skills of the children:

1. For younger kids, make a stencil for them by cutting a leaf shape out of tagboard for them using an Exacto™ knife. Tape the stencil to the tile and have them paint it.

2. For a more expressive look, have the kids draw the whole plant with a permanent marker and paint in the details.

3. You may wish to paint the whole tile with one color, wait for it to dry and draw a plant or plant part on it using another color.

Be sure to write the name of the plant below the drawings.

To assemble: Glue on clothespins to the back side of the tile so that the clasping part is aligned with the bottom of the tile (see illustration) and the clothespins are about 1/2 inch away from either side of the tile.

Copy a recipe onto a card (for a wild edible gift, of course!) and your new tile holder is ready as a gift or to keep your own cards handy.

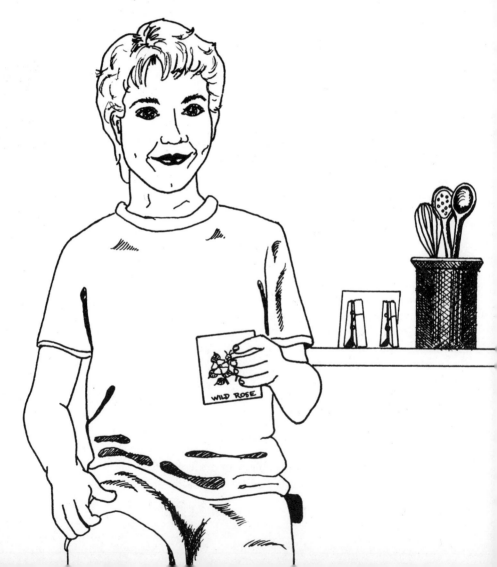

PLANTWORKS PLANTERS

To grow plantain and other wild edibles

Start your own patch of wild edibles in these recycled planters! By actually cultivating these kinds of plants, you are making a statement about their value and may help change their image from weed to vegetable. You'll also have a plant handy for you when you want to cook! The plants we suggest in this activity can be found in sidewalk cracks and in lawns, so you are not disturbing a wild area by digging up a whole plant.

Our choices of containers are designed to help your group remember the names of Plantworks plants. Who can forget purslane after they've planted it in a purse? Be creative and come up with your own planters that will reinforce plant names.

General directions: When digging up these plants, be sure to get the entire root system. Line the bottom of the containers with a layer of stones for drainage, then fill with soil. Pack the soil firmly around the roots and water well.

Purslane Purse

What you'll need:
old purse
potting soil
stones
purslane

Here's how:

Cost

Time

Ages
8 & up

Use an old purse near the cobweb stage. Place or hang on a porch or balcony.

Red Clover Cup

What you'll need:

plain ceramic mug
contact paper
potting soil
gravel or small pebbles
red clover plant
permanent marker

Cost
UNDER
$2 *per*
mug

Time
20
MINS.

Trace and cut clover leaf shapes out of contact paper, using the
illustration on p. 90 as a guide. Stick on mug in decorative way.
With a permanent marker write "Red clover, *Trifolium pratense*"
under the leaves.

Woolly Lamb's Quarter Pot

What you'll need:

scrap yarn
scissors
old flower pot
white glue
potting soil
lamb's-quarter plants.

Cost
UNDER
$2 *per*
pot

Time
1
HOUR

Here's how:

Cut a variety of lengths of yarn. Roll them into coils and brush one
side with white glue. Glue these buttons of yarn onto the cleaned
surface of the planter so that there is very little space in between
each yarn button. No gravel will be needed if the planter already
has holes in the bottom of it.

Plantain Planter

What you'll need:

old leather shoe
potting soil
pebbles
long shoelaces

Here's how:

From the natural history section, you'll remember that this plant was brought to North America with the European immigrants. Its nickname of "whiteman's foot" will be easily remembered in a man's old shoe. Water once a week and keep in filtered sunlight. For extra fun, paint the shoe in bright colors and use long shoelaces to hang it from the ceiling.

Cost
per shoe UNDER $2

Time
30 MINS

Ages 6 & up

OWL REFRIGERATOR MAGNETS

Cost

UNDER $2 *per owl*

Time

1 HOUR

Ages
10 & up

What you'll need:

acorn caps
white glue
sunflower seeds
felt
strip magnets
corrugated cardboard
toy eyes

Here's how:

In advance, draw owl shape onto cardboard and cut it out. Glue on acorn caps for the eyes and sunflower seeds (pointing toward the feet) for the wings and body. Cut out felt for beak and feet. Glue on cardboard owl. Glue magnet strip on the back of the owl and let dry.

"I MADE IT MYSELF" JELLY JAR

Decorate jelly jars to fill with the homemade jellies you can make (see pp. 36, 47, 51, 52, and 53). They make great gifts for friends or relatives.

What you'll need:

jelly jar
scrap piece of tightly woven decorative cotton fabric
tree tags (get from your local nursery)
white glue
potpourri
small wicker basket

Cost
UNDER
$5

Time
15
MINS.

Ages
9 & up

Here's how:

Before boiling the jar and lid, trace the lid onto the fabric and cut out the shape.

After the jar and lid have been boiled, filled and sealed (see jelly-making directions, pp. 34-35), brush glue onto the back of the fabric circle and press it onto the lid. Allow to dry. Mark the tree tag, "[name]'s home-made sumac jelly" and twist it into place under the lid. Place the jar in a basket layered with potpourri and tie a ribbon on the basket. Encourage the receiver to reuse the jar and basket when they finish the jelly.

SPICES IN A SHOEBOX

Cost

UNDER $10 *per set*

Time

30 MINS.

Ages 5-12

With all of the cooking you've been doing, wouldn't it be great to have all of the spices you need in labeled containers? This craft not only gives film containers and shoeboxes a second life, it makes spices very portable for camping.

What you'll need:

1	small shoebox or cardboard box
5-7	empty plastic film containers (clear ones are preferable)
5-7	self sticking labels
	permanent marking pen
5-7	plastic spice lids for film containers
	(can be purchased at camping stores)
	magazine pictures of prepared food
	"Mod Podge" (available in craft stores)
	white glue
	spices (salt, black pepper, garlic powder, chives, cinnamon, seasoned salt, rosemary, thyme, etc.)

Here's How:

Thoroughly wash and dry the film containers. Put in your spices and label each one. The pre-made labels will have to be cut in order to fit on the containers. For younger kids who haven't learned to read yet, establish a color which represents each spice and have them color code their spices.

Next decorate shoe box with cut-out pictures of food from a cooking magazine. Glue them on both the bottom and lid of the box. Brush on a protective coating of non-toxic Mod Podge over the pictures. Store your spices in your newly decorated box. Write your name on a large label and put in on the outside of the box, for example, "Larry's Spicebox."

A TOEFUL OF POTPOURRI

Cost
UNDER
$5 *each*

Time
1
HOUR
*each
step,*
over 3 weeks

*Ages
9 & up*

Plan to do this activity over the course of several weeks in the late summer, a few steps at a time. It's a fun way to make clothing drawers smell great. Potpourri means a mixture of many different things, so use any combination of flowers you want—we do suggest, however, that you use garden flowers to make up the bulk of the contents. Dry some wild rose petals and add to the garden mixture. For color, add dried sumac seeds. For shape, leave some flowers whole, like roses and marigolds. Thoroughly dehydrated fruits may also be added to your potpourri mixture for texture.

As a short cut, or for use with younger children, pick and dry some wild rose petals and add them to store bought potpourri. The following instructions are for making potpourri from scratch.

What you'll need:

1 pair	old, washed panty hose for every two children.
12-15"	lacy ribbon per child
6 cups	dried flowers

(consider red clover and dandelion flowers and curled dock seeds)

Spices:
1/4 cup	cinnamon
1/4 cup	cloves
1/4 cup	allspice

Fixative (choose one):
1 cup	gum arabic (found in drug stores)
or 1/8 cup	crushed orris root (found in many food co-ops)

Oils (choose one or mix):
1/8 oz   rose oil
1/8 oz   lemon oil
1/8 oz   cinnamon oil
or 1/8 oz   orange oil (our favorite)
(look for these in specialty floral shops or food co-ops)

Here's how:

Step 1, *Drying the flowers:* Remove the petals from the flowers and lay them out to dry on an absorbent towel. During the next week, turn them over several times until they are thoroughly dry. If not completely dry, they will mold!

Step 2, *Mixing the ingredients:* In a large bowl (make sure it has a cover that fits), mix all of the ingredients together. Cover the bowl and let it stand for one or two weeks.

Step 3, *Filling:* Cut off panty hose just below the heel. Pour in approximately 2 tablespoons of the mixture into the toe. Tie the opening with the ribbon. Give as a gift with a note listing the plants (wild or otherwise) you picked for the mixture.

WOODEN LEAF
CUTTING BOARD

When you want to make a very useful long-lasting craft that will make a great gift, this is the one to choose. You need to be handy with a jigsaw. We recommend broad leaves like the oak and basswood for this activity; they are easier to cut with a jigsaw.

Cost

UNDER
$5   *per board*

Time

2
HOURS

What you'll need:

1 length	1 x 12 pine board (Actually about 3/4" thick x 11 1/4" wide). Length should be determined by the size of the leaf you choose to draw.
1	enlarged leaf shape from p. 111 cut out of paper, about 8 1/2 x 11 (use a photocopy machine that enlarges or draw one freehand)
	scissors
	pencil
	sandpaper, medium and fine
	jigsaw
	tack cloth
	mineral oil (do not use varnish if this is to be used with food. If it will be used only as a decorative piece, you may wish to use a glossy polyurethane finish.)

Ages
10 & up

Here's how:

Trace leaf-shape onto board. Have an adult cut out leaf shape with jigsaw. Sand all sides and edges of the board with medium grade sandpaper. Sand again with fine grade sandpaper. Wipe off all sawdust with tack cloth. Rub with mineral oil. As a finishing touch wood burn or write the name of the leaf including the Latin name on the bottom of the cutting board. These make special gifts or great boards for future cooking excursions.

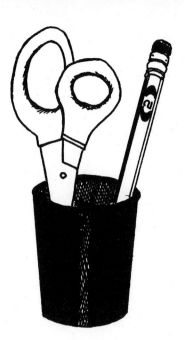

AMERICAN BASSWOOD
Tilia americana

MAKE A FOOD DEHYDRATOR

Here's a craft that's more involved but it will extend the ways and seasons in which you can use wild edibles.

Cost
UNDER
$15
per person

Time
3
HOURS
(some groups take all day)

Ages
12 & up

What you'll need:

1	4x8' 1/2" plywood sheet
1	handle
1 roll	window screen
2	door hinges
2-3 dozen	1 1/2" finishing nails
1	100-watt light bulb
1	light fixture, cord and switch
	hammer
	wood saw
	staple gun.

Here's how:

Start by laying out the plywood on the floor, drawing out the pattern. Allow a 1/4" space between pieces for the saw cuts. Cut out all parts. Measure and mark off the line on the inside of the sides where the shelf supports are to be attached. Attach the top and bottom to the sides with the nails as shown in the illustration. The back board should be attached so as to give the most support. Allow an air space both above and below the back panel for a flow of air that will be drawn in and out of the dehydrator. Glue can be used at all the joints for more strength if desired. Attach small strips of wood to the inside of the sides to support the shelf. Allow enough room for the fixture and bulb.

Attach the door using the door hinges, allowing enough space both above and below the door to draw air in and out of the dehydrator. Screw the light fixture to the center of the bottom of the dehydrator.

Now make the square screen frames by either making a miter cut (45 degree cut) or butting the ends up against each other and attaching with staples. Measure the screening to overlap the edges of the frame and cut to size. Staple the screening in place. Slide the screen shelf into place and plug in the bulb.

The hot bulb will warm the air in the dehydrator, causing it to rise out the openings and drawing cool air in through the bottom. This exchange of air dries material on the shelves. To stop, just unplug.

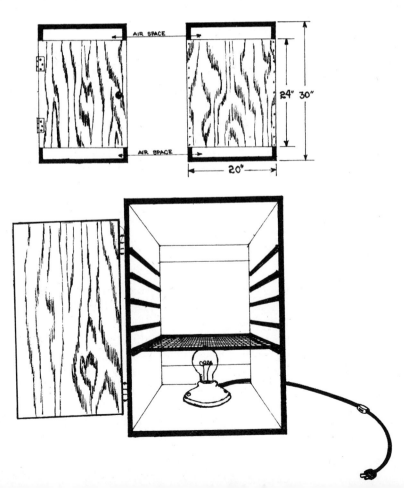

MAKE A MINI-PLANT PRESS

Use a plant press to preserve plants for study or future crafts. Remember to pick only what you need and never any protected rare plants.

Cost

UNDER $10 per pot

Time

2 HOURS

Ages
9 & up

What you'll need per press:

1	1' length of 1 x 4" pine board
4	4" bolts
4	wing nuts and washers
	wood drill and bit
	wood saw
	scissors
	string
	cardboard, cut from an old box
	newsprint

Here's how:

Cut the pine board into 6" lengths (you'll have two pieces per press).

For each press: Hold or clamp the two boards together and drill four holes, one at each corner. Drill a fifth hole at the top to pass the string through. Be sure the holes are slightly larger than the bolts so they can pass easily through. Cut the cardboard and blotting paper to fit inside the two boards. Assemble the press like a sandwich, with the two cardboard pieces inside the wood and the paper inside the cardboard as in the illustration.

This assembled plant press can be carried around the shoulder by a string when you go for a hike. To press a plant, just loosen up the wing nuts, place the plant you want to press between the blotter paper, and tighten the wing nuts. The plant will dry in anywhere from overnight to three days.

Notes

You may use 1/4" plywood, but more cutting will be needed to cut the wood into 4 x 6" pieces.

If an adult cuts the wood, younger children can do this project.

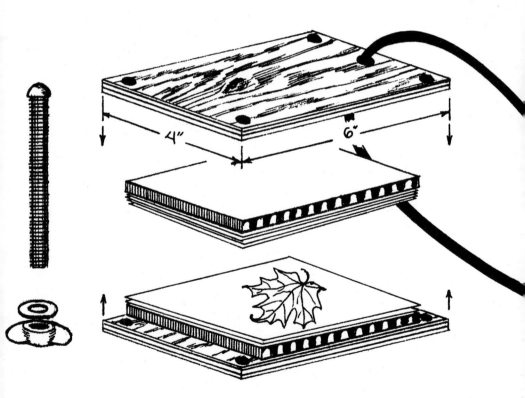

WOVEN CATTAIL MATS

Many uses were found for the versatile cattail plant long before Europeans "discovered" North America. See natural history pp. 76-77.

Cost
UNDER $2

Time
1 HOUR

Ages
9 & up

What you'll need:

20-30 cattail leaves
masking tape

Here's how:

Since cattails shrink when dried, collect them and let dry in a sunny place for one day. Before starting the mats, soak the leaves in water to make them pliable

Cut the leaves into equal lengths, a bit larger than you want the final mat to be. On a table, lay out a layer of parallel cattail leaves about inch apart from each other to the width you want your mat to be. Fasten these down to table at one end with masking tape. Weave one leaf at a time perpendicular to these leaves, alternating over and under with under and over, until you are satisfied with the mat's size. As you weave, be sure the leaves are packed densely enough to hold the mat together.

Depending on how the mat will be used, you can finish the edges by hemming them with a strip of cloth, or by folding the ends back over the last leaf they crossed, then under the leaf before that, forming a loop. Cattail mats are durable; use them under pots of wild edible plants!

GLOSSARY

Plant terms

ALIEN. No, this does not refer to creatures from outer space, but plants from across the ocean. That is, plants which evolved in Europe or Asia and were brought to the continental U.S. by accident or on purpose and have escaped into the wild.

ALTERNATE. A type of leaf attachment where the petioles are attached so that they are not across from one another.

ASYMMETRICAL. If you were to divide a leaf in half and one half had a different shape than the other, it would be asymmetrical.

BASAL LEAVES. The basal leaves attach to the plant at the bottom of its stem near to the ground.

BIENNIAL. A plant that takes two years to reach its flowering stage.

CHEVRON. A V-like marking.

COMPOUND LEAF. A leaf divided into several parts which are called leaflets.

DECIDUOUS. Trees which lose all or most of their leaves at a certain season.

DISTURBED AREAS. Land which has been recently unearthed or changed by grazing, fire or clear-cutting.

DRUPE. Fleshy fruit with a single seed, e.g. sumac.

ENTIRE. A leaf with smooth edges, lacking teeth or lobes.

FAMILY. A group consisting of several genera of plants.

GENUS. A group of related plant (and animal) species. Usually of Latin or Greek origin.

INTRODUCED. A plant brought into an area by humans, where the plant is not native. (see alien)

LEAF AXIL. The angle between leaf petiole and stem.

LEAFLET. A leaf which is compound is divided into smaller subdivisions called leaflets.

LOBE. A division of a leaf.

MARGIN. The edge of the leaf.

MIDRIB. The larger middle vein of the leaf; divides the leaf in half.

OPENLANDS. Dry grassy areas including lawn, disturbed soils, vacant lots and gardens.

OPPOSITE. A leaf arrangement consisting of leaves opposing each other on a stem.

PETIOLE. The stalk of the leaf.

PHENOLOGY. The science which involves study of the seasonal timing of plant flowering, bird migration etc.

RHIZOME. An elongated underground horizontal stem.

SEPALS. Outer flower parts within a bud which function to protect an unopened flower, often resembling a green leaf.

SERRATED. Just like the serrated cutlery knives, this is a "toothed" edge of a leaf.

SHOOT. New young above-ground growth on a plant, as in stem and leaves.

SIMPLE LEAF. A single leaf without divisions or lobes.

SPECIES. A group of plants that share similar characteristics and can interbreed to produce fertile offspring; a kind of organism e.g. *Chenopodium album* (Lambs quarters). Species name usually describes something specific about the plant. e.g. *alba*=white.

STALK. The upright main stem of a fleshy plant.

STAMENS. The male parts of a flower; hairlike protrusions near the center of the flower which hold pollen at their tip.

STEM. The upright parts of a plant to which all of the leaves are attached.

SUCCESSION. Refers to the natural process of one type of vegetation turning into another type of vegetation over a long period of time, e.g. a meadow changing into a forest.

TANNIN. A bitter chemical produced by many green leafy plants as they age in order to protect them from being consumed.

TAPROOT. Vertical root structure forming a stout tapering main root with no apparent major branching.

TAXONOMY. A branch of botany which deals with the naming, description and classification of plants.

TENDRIL. The slender coiling part of vines which grasp onto other plants for support. Tendrils are usually modified leaves or parts of leaves.

TERMINAL. At the end of any structure.

TRANSITION. Shrubby growth areas which are at the edge or border of lake, forest, stream or prairie habitats exhibiting characteristics of two different areas.

WETLAND. Low-lying wet areas, sparsely populated with tall reed-like plants often bordering lakes and streams.

WOODLAND. Areas where the dominant plants are hardwood, deciduous trees as in oak and maple-basswood forests.

150

BLANCH. To steam or boil briefly.

CHEESE CLOTH. Store-bought loosely woven cotton gauze.

CHOPPED. Cut up into bite size pieces no smaller than a half dollar.

CHOPPED FINE. Cut up into small pieces no larger than a pea.

CUBED. Cut into small square about the size of a quarter.

FRY PAN. Typically 9"- 12" diameter pan, usually non-stick with handle.

FULL BOIL. Continues to boil even while stirring.

HARD BOIL. A continous boil lasting several minutes.

PARBOIL. To boil briefly, not cook throroughly.

PURÉE. To liquefy by putting in a blender at high speed.

REDUCE. To partially evaporate a liquid through boiling.

SAUCE PAN. Small deep pan with a handle, typically 1-2 quarts.

SAUTÉ. To fry lightly in butter.

SOFTEN BUTTER. Butter that is at room temperature or warmed in oven.

STEEP. To allow an herb to soak in near-boiling water.

TEA BALL. Small perforated metal ball that holds crushed tea leaves.

WHISK. The verb which means a process of using a whisk that whips the liquid with rapid motion.

BIBLIOGRAPHY

Angier, Bradford. *Field Guide to Edible Wild Plants*. Harrisburg, PA: Stackpole Books, 1974.

——. *Feasting Free on Wild Edibles*. Harrisburg, PA: Stackpole Books, 1972.

Bowes and Church's. *Food Values of Portions Commonly Used (14th edition)*. Philadelphia: J.B. Lippincott & Co, 1985.

Britton and Brown. *An Illustrated Flora of the Northern U.S. & Canada (Volumes I, II & III)*. New York: Dover Publications, 1970.

Brown, Tom. *Guide to Wild Edible and Medicinal Plants*. New York: Berkley Publishing Company, 1985.

Dykeman, Peter A. and Thomas S. Elias. *Field Guide to North American Edible Wild Plants*. New York: Outdoor Life, 1982.

Earthworks Groups. *50 Simple Things You Can Do To Save the Earth*. Berkeley, CA: Earthworks Press, 1989.

Fernald, Merritt Lyndon. *Gray's Manual of Botany (8th Edition)*. New York: Van Nostrand, 1970.

Gibbons, Euell. *Stalking the Faraway Places*. New York: David McKay, 1973.

——. *Stalking the Good Life*. New York: David McKay, 1971.

——. *Stalking The Wild Asparagus*. New York: David McKay, 1962.

—— and Gordon Tucker. *Handbook of Edible Wild Plants*. Virginia Beach, VA: Donning Company, 1979.

Gleason, Henry A. and Arthur Cronquist. *Manual of Vascular Plants Northeastern United States and Adjacent Canada*. Boston: Willard Grant Press, 1963.

Green Pages, The. Westminster, MD: Bennett Information Group, 1990.

Hall, Alan. *The Wild Food Trail Guide*. New York: Holt, Rinehart and Winston, 1973.

Haughton, Claire. *Green Immigrants*. Harcourt Brace Jovanovich, 1978.

Huxley, Anthony. *Green Inheritance*. Garden City, NY: Anchor Press/Doubleday, 1985.

Kelsey, Harland P. and William A. Dayton. *Standardized Plant Names (2nd edition)*. Harrisburg, PA: J. Horace McFarland, 1942.

Kingsbury, John M. *Poisonous Plants of the United States and Canada*. Englewood Cliffs, NJ: Prentice Hall, 1964.

March, Andrew L. and Kathryn G. March. *The Quest for Wild Jelly*. Bailey, CO: Meridian Hill Publications, 1981.

——. *The Wild Taste*. Bailey, CO: Meridian Hill Publications, 1989.

Peterson, Allen L. *A Field Guide to Edible Wild Plants: Eastern/ Central North America*. Boston: Houghton Mifflin, 1977.

Peterson, McKenny. *A Field Guide to Wildflowers*. Boston: Houghton Mifflin, 1968.

Phillips, Roger. *Wild Foods*. Boston: Little, Brown and Co., 1986.

Seymour, Frank C. *The Flora of New England*. Rutland, VT: Charles E. Tuttle, 1969.

Steere, William C. Editor. *Wildflowers of the United States: The Northeast States*. New York: McGraw-Hill.

Tatum, Billy J. *Wild Food Field Guide and Cookbook*. New York: Workman, 1976.

INDEX

ABOUT THE AUTHORS

Stan Tekiela has pursued a mixed area of interests with an emphasis on medical and botanical studies. Professionally, Stan has worked full time as an emergency paramedic for ten years and continues to enjoy the diversity only that job can bring. For the past thirteen years, Stan has been studying and teaching the values of wild edible plants to hundreds of students for a variety of nature centers and organizations in Minnesota.

Stan credits his parents for starting and supporting his love for the environment and cooking. When not out photographing plants, Stan spends his recreational time rock-climbing, whitewater kayaking and guiding trips into the wilderness of the Boundary Waters Canoe Area in northern Minnesota with his wife Katherine. Woodworking and furniture-building fill in his off-season. Currently, Stan is finishing a bachelor's degree in botany at the University of Minnesota.

Karen Shanberg is in her eighth year as an interpretive naturalist at Springbrook Nature Center in Fridley, Minnesota. She
develops and leads programs including classes on wild edibles
for hundreds of people of all ages each year. Karen has taken an
active role in helping to save the rain forest of Latin America.
In addition to leading an eco-tour to Costa Rica in 1991, she
brings her Amazon parrot, her boa constrictor, and her slides
to speaking engagements throughout the Minneapolis/St. Paul
area. In the past two years, her efforts have helped to purchase
and preserve more than fifty acres of rain forest.

Karen is active in several environmental and interpretive organizations. She chaired the Stewardship Outreach Committee
for Earth Day 1990 and the publicity committees for the Minnesota Naturalists' Association (1986-1989) and the National
Association of Interpreters 1989 conference. She is currently
active on the advisory boards of the Kids for Saving the Earth
organization and the Minnesota Earthday Network.

Karen received her masters degree in outdoor education and
recreation from the University of Minnesota, and holds a Minnesota teacher's certificate for grades one through six. In her
spare time, Karen is an avid scuba diver, photographer, cross-
country skier and camper. She lives with her husband Neil,
three snakes, a parrot and a dog in Crystal, Minnesota.

Notes

Notes

Notes

Notes

Notes

Notes

Notes

Notes